Churchill's German
Special Forces

By the same author

Pen and Sword

Axis of Evil: The War on Terror Edited with Gwyn Winfield (2005).

The Rhodesian War: A Military History (with Dr Peter McLaughlin) (2008)

Mugabe's War Machine (2011).

Total Destruction of the Tamil Tigers: The Rare Victory of Sri Lanka's Long War (2012).

Omar al-Bashir and Africa's Longest War (2015)

The Jihadist Threat: The Re-conquest of Europe? (2015)

Dying for the Truth: The Concise History of Frontline War Reporting (2016)

Superpowers, Rogue States and Terrorism: Countering the Security Threats to the West (2017)

Total Onslaught: War and Revolution in Southern Africa Since 1945 (2018)

Deadlines on the Front Line: Travels with a Veteran War Correspondent (2018)

North Korea: Warring with the World (2020)

Other non-fiction

A Short Thousand Years: The End of Rhodesia's Rebellion (College Press, 1979)

Stander: Bank Robber with Mike Cohen (Galago, 1984)

Inside the Danger Zones: Travels to Arresting Places (Biteback, 2010)

Shooting the Messenger: The Politics of War Reporting with Professor Phil Taylor (Potomac, 2008, updated paperback, Biteback, 2011)

It Just Doesn't Add Up: Explaining Dyscalculia and Overcoming Number Problems for Children and Adults (Tarquin, St Albans, 2015)

Fiction

Anchoress of Shere (Poisoned Pen Press, 2002)

Regression (Millstream, 2012)

Churchill's German Special Forces

The Elite Refugee Troops who took the War to Hitler

Paul Moorcraft

Pen & Sword
MILITARY

First published in Great Britain in 2023 by
Pen & Sword Military
An imprint of
Pen & Sword Books Ltd
Yorkshire – Philadelphia

ISBN 978 1 39906 128 5

Typeset by Mac Style
Printed in the UK by CPI Group (UK) Ltd, Croydon, CR0 4YY.

Pen & Sword Books Limited incorporates the imprints of Atlas,
Archaeology, Aviation, Discovery, Family History, Fiction, History,
Maritime, Military, Military Classics, Politics, Select, Transport, True
Crime, Air World, Frontline Publishing, Leo Cooper, Remember
When, Seaforth Publishing, The Praetorian Press, Wharncliffe Local
History, Wharncliffe Transport, Wharncliffe True Crime, White Owl
and After the Battle.

For a complete list of Pen & Sword titles please contact

PEN & SWORD BOOKS LIMITED
47 Church Street, Barnsley, South Yorkshire, S70 2AS, England
E-mail: enquiries@pen-and-sword.co.uk
Website: www.pen-and-sword.co.uk

Or

PEN AND SWORD BOOKS
1950 Lawrence Rd, Havertown, PA 19083, USA
E-mail: Uspen-and-sword@casematepublishers.com
Website: www.penandswordbooks.com

Contents

'*Professor Moorcraft's book expertly re-tells in some detail some of a crucial hidden part of recent Jewish military history in World War Two, unknown even to many Jewish people, in an exciting, easy-to-read and engaging manner.*'

Martin Sugarman (Association of Jewish Ex-Servicemen archivist and author), the leading authority on Jewish men and women serving in the British armed forces during the Second World War.

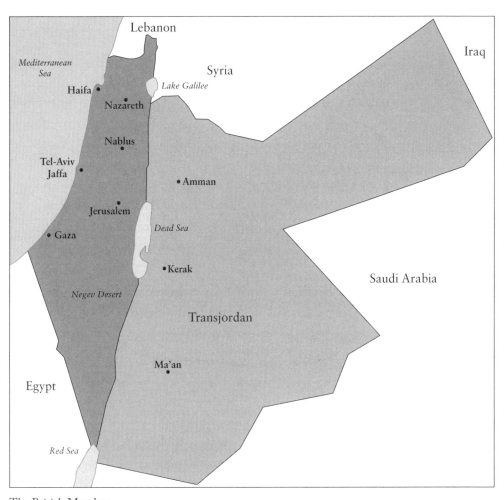

The British Mandate.

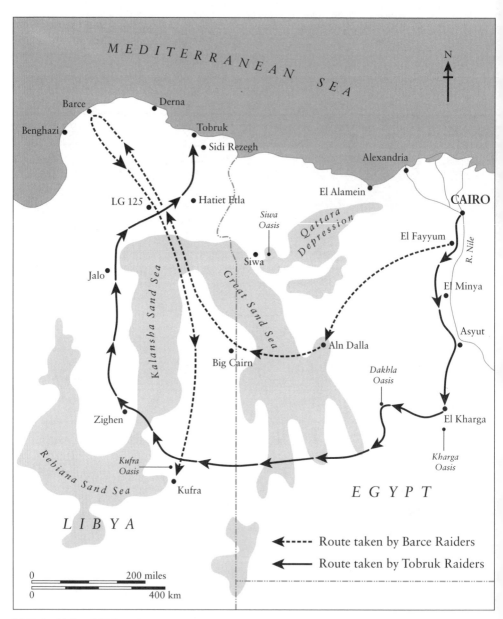

MEDITERRANEAN SEA

N

Barce
Benghazi
Derna
Tobruk
Sidi Rezegh
Alexandria
El Alamein
CAIRO
LG 125
Hatiet Etla
Siwa Oasis
Qattara Depression
El Fayyum
Jalo
Siwa
Great Sand Sea
Kalansha Sand Sea
El Minya
R. Nile
Asyut
Aln Dalla
Big Cairn
Dakhla Oasis
Zighen
El Kharga
Kufra Oasis
Rebiana Sand Sea
Kufra
Kharga Oasis
EGYPT

LIBYA

◀----- Route taken by Barce Raiders
◀—— Route taken by Tobruk Raiders

0   200 miles
0   400 km

LRDG, SAS and SIG raids from the desert.

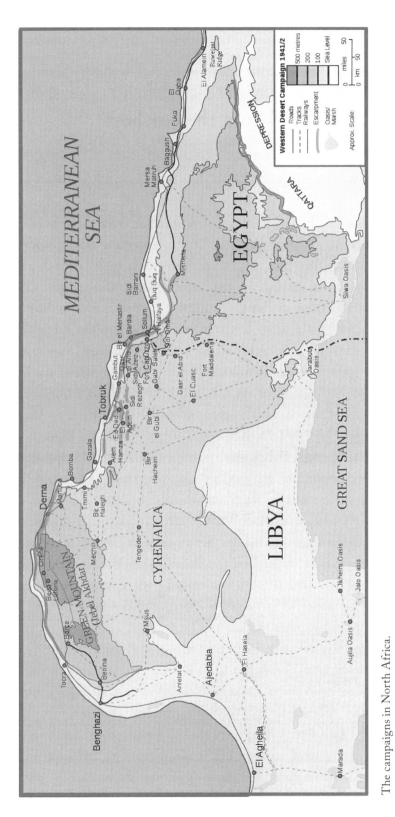

The campaigns in North Africa.

About the Author

Professor Paul Moorcraft has written over fifty books, both fiction and non-fiction. After completing his studies at six universities, he taught politics and international relations fulltime (consecutively) at ten international universities. He has held professorships in the USA and UK. In addition, he was a print and broadcast journalist in thirty war zones. Besides being a senior instructor for five years at the Royal Military Academy, Sandhurst, and then the Joint Services Command and Staff College (later the Defence Academy), he worked for the UK Ministry of Defence in the Balkans and Middle East, as well as reluctantly driving a desk in Whitehall on occasion. In 2004 Dr Moorcraft was the founder director of the Centre for Foreign Policy Analysis, London, a think tank dedicated to conflict resolution. He was, for example, Head of Mission for fifty British observers during the Sudan election in 2010.

The author has worked extensively behind 'enemy lines', most notably with the *Mujahedeen* during the Soviet occupation of Afghanistan. His book, *The Jihadist Threat*, was shortlisted as the British Army's military book of the year in 2016. He has worked with, and reported on, special forces in countries as far apart as Nepal and South Africa, as well as serving in Zimbabwe's forces. His early good command of German, and later some Hebrew, supported the initial research for this book. His knowledge of Welsh has been useful, too, as some of the Jewish commandos lived and trained in North Wales and indeed sometimes successfully claimed to be Welsh when captured (this was to disguise their often fractured English). He has also worked in desert war zones, most recently during six trips in Darfur, where he spent time with rebel groups and separately with Sudanese government forces.

Professor Moorcraft's best known novel is *Anchoress of Shere*, which won awards in the USA. He has done extensive pro bono charity work, for example as a consultant for disabled people travelling on UK railways and for ten years did part-time charity work for the five million dyscalculics in the UK; his book on the subject, *It Just Doesn't Add Up*, has gone into numerous editions.

A Fellow of the Royal Historical Society, in 2021 he returned to Wales to live in the seaside town of Penarth, in the Vale of Glamorgan.

Acknowledgements

One of my most important sources has been Martin Sugarman, not only his magisterial work, *Fighting Back*, but also his personal advice and insights not least from his time working in the Jewish Military Museum. Another London advisor has been James Barker. He is an authority on the British Mandate in Palestine, as well as being a general military expert from his time working in the Imperial War Museum. He kindly read the manuscript before publication.

In Wales, I would like to thank Anne Markham at the Tywyn Library, and Elaine Roberts of the Dolgellau Record Office. Also, Wendy Gruffydd showed me around some of the commando sites near Aberdyfi and helped with translations from the Welsh. All were very patient, not least with my determined but sometimes stuttering attempts to work in Welsh. Bob Tyrrell helped me in Aberdyfi as did Myra Hayler who deployed her immaculate Welsh and immaculate memory despite being, as she put it, 'ninety-nine and three-quarters'. Another Welsh connection, by descent, is Nerys Pipkin, the daughter of Captain Bryan Hilton-Jones, the OC of X Troop. She shared cherished memories of this amazing commando officer and helped with pictures and access to her father's correspondence. On Sark, Lieutenant Colonel (Retd) Reg Guille and Sue Guille helped with my enquiries about Operation BASALT. Yoram Gideoni helped with some background in Israel and my Hebrew translations. Friends read initial drafts including John Sayce. Another friend who asked whether I had actually reported on the Second World War will not be mentioned. In fact, this is practically my first non-fiction book I have written that is not based on my own eye-witness experiences in war zones. And I could not travel very much to research archives not because of my nearly complete blindness but because of the damn Covid pandemic.

This is my thirteenth book for Pen and Sword; I hope it is not unlucky. So far, I *have* been lucky in the support of the publishing director, Brigadier (Retd) Henry Wilson, the ever-helpful production manager, Matt Jones, and the best editor an author could want: Richard Doherty, a better historian than I will ever be.

Notes on Cover

The main front cover picture is of Long Range Desert Group Chevrolet 30-cwt trucks; the front right flap shows Rommel talking to his men in a captured American half-track during the fighting in Tunisia.

The back cover pictures from left to right show Captain Bryan Hilton-Jones, CO of X Troop, next door is Maurice Tiefenbrunner and the Jewish Brigade soldier with the shell (which says in Hebrew 'a gift to Hitler') is Joseph Wald.

The three Jewish soldiers together are Dov Cohen, Philip Kogel and Dolph Zeintner, still in their Middle East 51 Commando uniform. Note the unit sign on the hat. They were on leave before joining the SIG. Picture on bottom right: Operation AGREEMENT, 'C Commando Force'.

Timeline – North African Campaign

1940

10 June: Italy declares war on France and the UK

July: Royal Navy shells French warships in the port of Oran to keep them out of German hands

13 September: Italian forces invade Egypt from Libya

16 September: Italian forces establish front east of Sidi Barrani

10 December: Indian forces capture Sidi Barrani

16 December: Sollum retaken by British forces

1941

January: Bardia captured by British and Australian troops

6 January: Tobruk captured by British and Australian forces

February: Fall of Benghazi to Western Desert Force. Lieutenant-General Erwin Rommel is appointed commander of *Deutsches Afrikakorps*

7 February: What remains of the Italian Tenth Army surrenders

9 February: Churchill orders halt to British and Australian advance at El Agheila to allow withdrawal of troops to defend Greece

14 February: First units of the *Afrikakorps* under Erwin Rommel start to arrive in Libya

24 March: British forces at El Agheila defeated; Erwin Rommel starts his advance.

4 April: British forces withdraw from Benghazi

10 April: Siege of Tobruk by Axis begins

15 April: British forces are pushed back to Sollum on Egyptian border with Libya

30 April: Australian forces lose a small part of their positions in Tobruk during the Battle of the Salient; roughly a sixth of Tobruk is now held by Germans

16 May: Italian forces attack Australian forces in Tobruk, forcing them to withdraw

5 July: General Sir Claude Auchinleck replaces General Sir Archibald Wavell as Commander-in-Chief Middle East

15 August: German *Panzergruppe Afrika* activated with Rommel in command

10 September: Western Army formed by Auchinleck

18 September: German air raid on Cairo in which 39 Egyptian civilians are killed and nearly 100 injured, bringing condemnation against the Axis from the Arab press. Radio Berlin later apologises to its Arab listeners

25 September: Western Army redesignated Eighth Army

18 November: Auchinleck's Operation CRUSADER begins (18 November-30 December 1941) with British, Indian, New Zealand, Polish and South African forces

21 November: British armoured division defeated at Sidi Rezegh and withdraws

27 November: New Zealand troops at Sidi Azeiz defeated by overwhelming advance of Panzers and German infantry

28 November: 15th Panzer, despite being outnumbered 2:1, forces British tanks to retreat, exposing the New Zealand forces at El Duda on the Tobruk by-pass

1 December: New Zealand troops in Sidi Rezegh suffer heavy casualties from Panzers

9 December: Tobruk siege relieved by Eighth Army consisting of British, Indian, New Zealand, Polish and South African forces; White Knoll captured from elements of the Italian Brescia Division by the Polish Carpathian Brigade

24 December: British forces capture Benghazi

31 December: Front lines return to El Agheila

1942

21 January Rommel's second offensive begins

29 January: Benghazi captured by Axis forces

13 June: 'Black Saturday': Axis inflicts heavy defeat on Eighth Army on the Gazala line

21 June: Axis capture of Tobruk

28 June: Mersa Matruh, Egypt, falls to Rommel

29 June: American reports from Egypt of British military operations (which the Axis were reading) stopped

30 June: Axis forces reach El Alamein and attack British positions, the First Battle of El Alamein begins

13 August: Generals Alexander and Montgomery take charge respectively of Middle East Command and Eighth Army

13 September: Allies launch unsuccessful Operation AGREEMENT, a large-scale amphibious raid directed against Tobruk

23 October: Montgomery launches Operation LIGHTFOOT starting the final Battle of El Alamein (23 October-5 November 1942)

5 November: Axis lines broken at El Alamein

8 November: Operation TORCH is launched under command of General Eisenhower; Allied forces land in Morocco and Algeria

9 November: Sidi Barrani re-captured by Eighth Army

13 November: Tobruk re-captured by Eighth Army

15 November: British forces re-capture Derna, Libya

20 November: Benghazi re-captured by Eighth Army

12 December: Eighth Army starts an offensive towards Axis forces near El Agheila

25 December: Sirte captured by Eighth Army

1943

A re-unified French Army is created when the Army of Africa (*Armée d'Afrique*) led by General Giraud is combined with the Free French Forces (*Forces Françaises Libres*) of General de Gaulle

23 January: Tripoli captured by British Eighth Army

4 February: Axis forces in Libya retreat to Tunisian border south of the Mareth Line

19 February: Battle of Kasserine Pass launched by Axis forces

23 March: US II Corps emerge from Kasserine to match the Axis at Battle of El Guettar

7 May: British enter Tunis, Americans enter Bizerte

13 May: Last Axis troops surrender in Tunisia

Introduction: Fighting back

This book reveals the story of the secret German-speaking units that Winston Churchill helped to deploy in the Second World War. The majority were comprised of Germans but many native German-speakers from other countries such as Austria, Poland and Czechoslovakia were also recruited. Much of this story has long been top secret although more recently the commandos of X Troop have been written about. While the hidden units were nearly all made up of German-speaking Jews, these secret forces often had a sprinkling of non-Jewish personnel. An even more top-secret unit was the Special Interrogation Group. The SIG men were even more daring special forces who spoke German and, unlike the X Troops, fought – and usually died – wearing German Wehrmacht uniform.

The SIG was a very small unit, not exceeding more than fifty men. They performed amazing deeds, even on one occasion drawing German army pay while infiltrating Erwin Rommel's forces. It was a highly secret unit because, once Berlin discovered the existence of the SIG, an enraged Adolf Hitler ordered that all such *Untermenschen* in German uniform should be executed immediately – with only a temporary reprieve if the captives, under torture, might offer some useful intelligence. The Führer went into a rage if these Jewish special forces were mentioned.

The exploits of the Jewish X Troop of 10 Commando also sent Hitler into a murderous frenzy, although in one famous case Field Marshal Erwin Rommel protected two commandos who had been captured on the French coast in the lead-up to D Day in 1944. Hitler had declared that all captured commandos – even if dressed in full Allied uniforms – would be handed over to the *Sicherheitsdienst* (SD) for likely torture and inevitable execution.

The fate of Jews caught fighting in German uniform was even more brutal. Until recently many of the details of the SIG remained locked away.

This book also recounts how some of the SIG and X Troop survivors went on to join the British SAS, and then, unofficially, hunt Nazi fugitives in Europe after the German surrender. The Jewish Brigade also executed numerous Nazis after May 1945. This book traces how this determination to fight back infused the early intelligence units and the armed forces of Israel after independence in 1948.

Even today this tradition is important in the Israeli special forces. The *Fauda* TV series became immensely popular with both Israeli and Arab audiences, as well as in Europe and America. Special forces units spawned by the IDF have operated throughout the Middle East, most dramatically in Syria and Iran. The *Fauda* TV drama series concentrates on a *mista'arvim* – an Arabic-speaking undercover counter-terrorism unit – famous for deploying in Gaza and the West Bank. They dress and talk like Arabs and, to add to the TV realism, some of the actors are ex-SF soldiers themselves.

Most of this story, however, is about how the hatred of Nazism drove the Jewish elite soldiers in the 1940s but the contemporary reflections only serve to enhance a spine-tingling legacy of courage and determination told here, often for the first time, in graphic and occasionally gory detail.

Chapter One

The First Modern Jewish Armies

A Jewish army?

How far should historians go back? Orde Wingate, one of the most colourful characters in this story, chose to regress as far as the *Old Testament*. In the 1930s the eccentric British officer set up the base for his Special Night Squads in Ein Harod, a Jewish settlement in the British mandate of Palestine. His choice was no accident – this is where the '300 men of Israel' were chosen by Gideon to fight the Midianites. Wingate saw himself as a latter-day Gideon in his passion for the Zionist cause.

What T.E. Lawrence achieved in the desert, his distant kin – Orde Wingate – achieved in the jungle, as leader of the Chindits in Burma. Wingate, however, had already cut his teeth as an Arabist in Sudan where he learned some of the skills of desert warfare. Nevertheless, when he arrived in Palestine in 1936, he rapidly became a convinced supporter of the Zionist cause. He taught himself to speak fluent Hebrew and often quoted at length – and accurately – from the *Old Testament*.

Above all, Wingate believed in the formation of a Zionist army to defend the Jewish minority in Palestine. The British Empire had been mandated the territory by the League of Nations in 1923 as part of the post-Great War carve-up, with the French, of the Middle East. British-led armies had captured Jerusalem from the crumbling Ottoman Empire in December 1917. Whether or not the British Empire should sponsor a purely Jewish army was often debated in Whitehall. Besides innate British official anti-Semitism, Arab sensitivities, especially in Palestine, were often factored in.

The Zionist movement looked to Britain to help create a homeland in Palestine. It had been suggested that a 'Jewish Rhodesia' could be set up in British East Africa but ardent Zionists wanted nothing short of Zion – Jerusalem as the capital of a new state. When General Sir Edmund Allenby took the holy city on 11 December 1917, the British premier, David Lloyd George, a Welshman steeped in biblical history, proclaimed it to be the best Christmas present of the war. A month before, on 2 November, the British foreign secretary, Arthur Balfour, sent a letter to Lord Rothschild, a prominent leader of the British Jewish community. In his letter Balfour declared that his country was sympathetic to the Zionist cause and said that the government favoured the establishment of a national home for the Jewish people in Palestine, though a condition was added that the non-Jewish majority was not to be disadvantaged.

This Balfour Declaration was to lead eventually to the foundation of the state of Israel in 1948. Before that, however, the Zionist dream was to inspire much bloodshed in Palestine between the Arab majority and the small but rapidly growing Jewish minority.

The demand for a modern Jewish nation state had largely originated in 1896 when Theodor Herzl's book *Der Judenstaat* was published in Vienna. The book generated extremes of wild enthusiasm and hostility (as well as widespread indifference) in the Jewish communities in Europe. It is worth quoting a contemporary story about two venerable Viennese rabbis sent to Palestine to explore the validity of Herzl's ideas. The fact-finding mission resulted in a cable sent from Palestine by the two rabbis: 'The bride is beautiful but she is married to another man.' Sadly, this is an apocryphal story. It does, however, capture the enduring dilemma of Jewish-Arab relations in Palestine/Israel.

The Great War

In 1917 two Jewish activists, Ze'ev Jabotinsky and Joseph Trumpeldor, played a significant role in creating the first Jewish *fighting* force, the Jewish Legion, as part of the British Army. Jabotinsky not only helped to form the Jewish Legion but his legacy lasted long after his death, especially in the formation of the powerful right-wing Zionist movement in opposition to the mainstream Zionist movement, which ultimately led to the Likud party in Israel. He was born in Odessa in 1880 as Vladimir Yevgenyevich Jabotinsky into a middle-class, assimilated and largely secular family. At 17 he became a journalist for his local Odessa newspaper. He then partied for three years in Rome rather than studying and so did not graduate. He did, however, become fluent in Italian as well as his native Russian with some Hebrew and conversational Yiddish.

Because of increasingly barbaric pogroms in Russia, Jabotinsky moved into serious journalism and dedicated political activism as a right-wing Zionist. He became an apostle of a Zionism that demanded control of all Palestine as well as the territories on both sides of the Jordan. He helped found the Jewish Self-Defence Organisation while he studied modern Hebrew and renamed himself Ze'ev (Wolf). Jabotinsky travelled from Russia to Istanbul to promote the Zionist cause and seek the help of the Sultan of Turkey who ruled over Palestine.

Joseph Trumpeldor, the most decorated Jewish soldier in the Tsarist army, had lost an arm defending Port Arthur in the Russo-Japanese war of 1904–5. Despite his disability he insisted on staying in the army. When the First World War broke out he was living in Palestine. As a Russian subject living in the Ottoman Empire, he was thus an enemy alien. He fled to Egypt, where, together with Ze'ev Jabotinsky, he developed the idea of a 'Jewish Legion' to fight alongside the British against the Turks in Palestine. Trumpeldor and Jabotinsky met General John Maxwell, the commander of British forces, in Cairo, on 15 March 1915 to discuss this idea. The general (a zealous amateur archaeologist who later became famous for his connection with the Tomb of Tutankhamun) explained that he could not enlist foreign nationals as fighting troops in the British Army. But he said he could let them join a volunteer transport mule corps.

Jabotinsky said no, but Trumpeldor said yes and immediately started recruiting both local-born Jews in Egypt and many recent Russian emigres from Palestine. Around 650 men joined the Zion Mule Corps of whom 562 finally served, and usually with gallantry, in the Gallipoli campaign after just a few weeks' training. They were armed with rifles and bayonets and were expected to fight as well as support logistics. This was considered to be the first all-Jewish military unit organised in almost two thousand years, since the Kochba revolt of 132–135 CE. It was the ideological beginning of the Israel Defence Forces. Trumpeldor, the second in command, saw action in Gallipoli where he was wounded in the shoulder but refused to leave the battlefield. The commander of the corps, Lieutenant Colonel John Henry Patterson, an Irish Protestant, later wrote that many of his men were fearless under heavy fire 'while Captain Trumpeldor actually revelled in it, and the hotter it became the more he liked it'. Trumpeldor was soon to die a hero's death in Tel Hai in northern Palestine in 1920. He had previously tried and failed to persuade the provisional government in Russia in 1917 to form a Jewish regiment in the Russian army which could fight its way through the Ottomans to reach Palestine.

Trumpeldor's unit, the Zion Mule Corps, had already returned from Gallipoli to Alexandria in January 1916 where it was disbanded two months later. But the legacy of the corps was important. Its commanding officer, Lieutenant Colonel Patterson, was a big-game hunter and an engineer (and also the author of the famous *The Man-Eaters of Tsavo*, that inspired three major films). He was, in addition, a Christian Zionist who later became a senior officer in the Jewish Legion.[1]

After the dissolution of the Zion Mule Corps, Ze'ev Jabotinsky and Trumpeldor led some 120 members of the Mule Corps to serve together in 16 Platoon of 20th Battalion The London Regiment, a Territorial Force unit that was expanded because of the demands of the Western Front. On 17 August 1917 a Jewish battalion was formally announced and was later designated as 38th Battalion Royal Fusiliers. The unit included some British volunteers as well as survivors of the Zion Mule Corps, plus some Russian Jewish emigres. In April 1918 it was joined by the 39th Battalion which had been raised at Fort Edward in Nova Scotia, Canada; these volunteers, unsurprisingly, came largely from North America. The unit, originally stood up in 1917, comprised around 1,100 men, including the future Israeli prime minister, David Ben Gurion.

A 40th Battalion was added which consisted largely of Palestinian Jewish volunteers, plus nearly 100 Ottoman Jewish PoWs. The other two battalions of the legion, the 41st and 42nd, were depot battalions stationed in England, at Plymouth. The total strength of the Jewish Legion was 5,000. Most of the recruits came from the USA, England and Palestine. In his memoirs, Jabotinsky noted that a further one per cent were Ottoman ex-prisoners and one per cent came from Argentina.

The Jewish Legion saw action in the final stages of Allenby's campaign in the Middle East. The 38th Battalion, serving alongside 31 Brigade of 10th (Irish) Division, fought about twenty miles north of their beloved Zion – Jerusalem. Many saw this as part of biblical revelations of the re-founding of Israel. The Legion also fought in the Battle of Megiddo, with all the religious echoes of the final battle of Armageddon, in September 1918. This was considered to be one of the decisive actions on the Ottoman front.

General Edmund Allenby, the commander of the Egyptian Expeditionary Force, achieved a great deal with very few casualties – unlike most of the great offensives of the First World War. He deployed creeping barrages/bombardments to cover set-piece infantry tactics that avoided trench warfare and then used mobile forces – especially his cavalry, armoured cars and aircraft – to encircle the Ottoman troops in Palestine. Also, Lawrence's Arab irregulars played a dynamic role, not least in terrorising the Turks – the Arabs often refused to take prisoners and sometimes massacred isolated outposts and stragglers. Allenby's plan for the Battle of Megiddo was brilliantly executed, despite a lack of manpower – 60,000 of the men under his command were suddenly (though temporarily) siphoned off to face the German final offensive on the Western Front. Allenby's strategy was not like anything else tried in France until the final 100 days of the war; rather it looked forward in style to the German *Blitzkrieg* of 1939/40.

In his history of the Ottoman army, *Ordered to Die,* Edward Erickson wrote

The Battle of the Nablus Plain ranks with Ludendorff's Black Days of the German Army in the effect that it had on the consciousness of the Turkish General Staff. It was now apparent to all but the most diehard nationalists that the Turks were finished in the war.

In spite of the great victories in Armenia and in Azerbaijan, Turkey was now in an indefensible condition…It was also apparent that the disintegration of the Bulgarian Army at Salonika and the dissolution of the Austro–Hungarian Army spelled disaster and defeat for the Central Powers. From now until the Armistice, the focus of the Turkish strategy would be to retain as much Ottoman territory as possible.[2]

The Turkish defeat in Palestine was exactly what the Zionists wanted. Jabotinsky was active in the Transjordan fighting that helped to bring about the final victory around Damascus. Despite his efforts to persuade the British to keep the Legion in Palestine, most of the Jewish soldiers were demobilised after the armistice in November 1918. The Legion was reduced to one battalion called 'the First Judeans' with their own distinctive cap badge adorned with a menorah. The cap badge also had 'forward' written on it in Hebrew but the dream of a cohesive Jewish army was to go into reverse gear for a long time. It was a small comfort for Jabotinsky but in December 1919 he was appointed MBE by the King.

The Rise of the Third Reich

This story is concerned primarily with the Jews who wanted to fight back against Nazism and often did so by joining British and US-led forces. Unlike in Poland, most German Jews were assimilated in 1933. They thought of themselves as Germans first and Jews second. Only the Zionists or the orthodox minority felt they were indeed different and/or felt they belonged elsewhere. Some young and idealistic Jews were attracted to communism and hundreds volunteered to fight in the International Brigades in the Spanish Civil War. A smaller number of Jews did join the small and scattered German resistance to Hitler but most were soon imprisoned or killed. A few more survived by connections with communist organisations and were spirited away to the USSR.

Those who really wanted to fight back by bearing arms had to emigrate. Except for the well-connected, many young Jewish would-be fighters were shabbily treated in England. Robert Kronfeld, an Austrian, was one of the exceptions: he was rapidly fast-tracked to be a squadron leader in the Royal Air Force (after the Nazis banned Jews from flying). He was internationally famous, however, as the holder of international glider records as well as being the first to fly a glider over the English Channel and back in the same day. He was a glider (and sea-plane) designer as well, and the RAF needed people like Kronfeld for the new fleets of military gliders.

Most aspiring Jewish fighters, however, had to run obstacle courses as 'aliens' who could join pioneer companies set up in 1939/40. Gradually the process improved, especially on rules regarding naturalisation. And then suddenly, as the war intensified, young German-speaking Jews, men and a few women outside medical services, who wanted to fight and could pass the rigorous fitness tests, were in demand both in Britain and America. Winston Churchill was one of the earliest converts to the role of Jewish anti-Nazi warriors. Not all the Jewish volunteers used arms to fight back, however. Many served in the BBC, for example, broadcasting to Europe or interpreting Nazi signals. As the war developed many more were used for interrogating prisoners and in intelligence gathering generally and then as post-war administrators and Nazi hunters in liberated Germany.

Nazi persecution in Germany after 1933 led inexorably to the rise of Jewish immigration – much of it illegal – into Palestine. Most Zionists regarded the British as potential saviours after the Balfour Declaration and as real allies after 1933 and then during the war against the Third Reich. After 1936, relations between Arab and Jews in Palestine degenerated into a low-level civil war. Most moderate Jewish organisations tried to work with the British, not least in military and police roles, especially after the British White Paper in April 1939; this restricted Jewish immigration and land purchases. Hard-line Zionists, such as the Irgun group, decided that their only course of action was to drive out the British mandate authority as the necessary precursor to an independent Jewish state.

Wingate

On 7 September 1936 an intelligence officer, with the rank of captain GS03 'I' with 5th Division, was posted to Haifa. This officer was Orde Wingate, who, despite his very scruffy demeanour, soon made his mark in both Palestine and in London, where Winston Churchill became a fan. Wingate was, frankly, weird. He was a naturist who never bathed but instead scraped his body with a stiff brush. He sometimes greeted visitors, even the most conservative of orthodox Jews, wearing nothing but his famous pith helmet and a fly-whisk. He ate raw onions for pleasure and also chewed oranges whole. But he later became a famous general, as did many other officers who served in the mandate between 1936 and 1939 – Bernard Montgomery and Archibald Wavell were two well-known, if arguably less eccentric, contemporaries.

Many British Army officers at the time were anti-Semitic and often strongly pro-Arab, especially those who had served in the Middle East and even more so if they had worked with the Foreign Office and the Colonial Office, though the anti-Jewish sentiment never reached the levels of bigotry that divided the French army in the 1890s during the infamous Dreyfus affair.

The 'Report on the Military Lessons of the Arab Rebellion in Palestine 1936' (War Office document 282/6, p. 117), mainly drafted by General Robert Haining (GOC Palestine 1938–39), said:

> The Jewish Police, in company with the rest of the Jews, suffered from a conviction which seemed to be firmly held by every British official without practical experiences that no Jew was of any use for fighting purposes. It was a curious thing that the type of Englishman who credited every Arab town lounger with the attributes of a Bedouin warrior would not hesitate to class the toughest German immigrant with the old-fashioned ringleted Jew of the ghetto. The falsity of this view was plainly demonstrated to the Army by the work of the Jews who drove most of the military transport in 1936, while the records of 1914–18 might well have provided further proof; but nevertheless in other quarters the conviction persisted.

This was a long-lasting paradox. Sometimes Jews were portrayed by the British imperialists as useless fighters but at other times, especially regarding the formation of a large Jewish army in Palestine, they were considered a major military threat.

So Wingate's passion for Zion was even more unusual in that he was a fluent Arabic-speaker who had read the Koran diligently. The British habit of recruiting so-called martial races, especially in the Raj, also applied to the Middle East where the alleged military prowess of the Bedouin was often lionised. Wingate's ambition to create a Jewish army in Palestine, allied with the Empire, ran counter to popular and official opinion in the mandate (and the Colonial Office), though Captain Wingate did have sympathisers among some of his peers in the officer corps and a few of his superiors in the top brass. Wingate reached high rank despite an eccentricity that bordered on showmanship. Eventually, Wingate's partisanship accelerated his removal from his Palestine post.

One example of his famous support for the Jews was when he was lunching with the Bishop of Jerusalem. An elderly British lady, sitting next to Wingate, said: 'If you are so fond of the Jews why don't you become one yourself?'

Modestly casting down his eyes, Wingate replied: 'Alas, I am not circumcised.'

In order to permit Jews who lived in remote rural settlements to defend themselves, the British established the Jewish Supernumerary Police force of 3,000 men (with 2,400 reservists). Most Arabist British officers thought this was going too far and argued that the imperial authorities would be perceived as taking sides.

With the unofficial co-operation of the moderate Jewish defence organisations, especially the Haganah, the clandestine local Jewish army, Wingate trained and led the Special Night Squads. They consisted of Jewish volunteers, including some who had served in European armies, though the officers and senior NCOs were usually British. Jewish volunteers helped with planning and training and did much of the fighting. Previously, Jewish police had operated from police stations that were monitored closely by the Arabs. Instead, Wingate based his men in the Jewish settlements and *kibbutzim*. They were well-trained and highly motivated and usually efficient. They were not 'cowboy' outfits: the Special Night Squads worked in tandem with local British regular brigades' counter-insurgency strategy.

Wingate recruited about 100 men including famous future Israeli commanders such as Moshe Dayan and Yigal Allon. Most came from the existing police or from Haganah commandos. They fought against Arab rebels, especially those attacking Jewish settlements in Galilee or sabotaging railways and road convoys and especially the vital Haifa-Mosul pipeline.

Sir Hew Strachan, an eminent British historian, said the night squad methods were 'state terrorism'. The same had been said of the antecedents, such as the Gurkha units on the borders of the Raj and the Auxiliary Division of the Royal Irish Constabulary (the 'Auxies'). Wingate's methods were effective and eventually night squads, minus any Jews, were deployed by the regular army throughout the mandate. Wingate was ordered to stand down from command of the squads in October 1938. Although he was awarded the DSO in the same year, he was effectively told never to return to Palestine. His units were put on garrison and prison duties before being disbanded. Nevertheless, Wingate had achieved part of his ambition – Dayan *et al* were to form the nucleus of the future Israel Defence Forces.

In 1966 Field Marshal Bernard Montgomery told General Moshe Dayan that he considered Wingate to have been 'mentally unbalanced'. Monty added with characteristic bluntness: 'The best thing he ever did was get killed in a plane crash in 1944.'

The Anglo-American connection

Wingate had done much to implement the concept of an independent Jewish fighting force but, after the 1939 White Paper, many Zionists fell out of love with the British connection. Jabotinsky, always full of grand ideas, alternated between hostility and tactical affection. In the 1930s he had talked of 'evacuating' millions of Jews from Poland and other parts of Eastern Europe. Prophetically he warned, 'Catastrophe is approaching … . The volcano that will soon spew out its flames of extermination.' But, after April 1939, the British authorities in the Mandate started closing the doors on Jewish immigration and the Jewish purchase of land in Palestine. The British had downgraded the vision of the Zionist state into the thrice-promised land. The Jews and Arabs had been promised much for fighting against the Ottomans and then the French and British empires swallowed up most of the contested territories. In 1939 a desperate Jabotinsky had talked of linking up with his followers in the Irgun terror group to spearhead a Jewish revolt *against* the British authorities. Once the war had begun, however, by 1940 Jabotinsky was offering the British Empire 130,000 Jewish volunteer soldiers.

The indefatigable Zionist died of a heart attack in New York on the night of 3/4 August 1940 while visiting a Jewish self-defence camp. Inevitably, he was in the middle of campaigning to raise an American Jewish army to fight the Nazis. About 40 per cent of America's 4.3 million Jews then lived in New York City and so were obvious targets for Jabotinsky. But many American Jews were keener on chasing the American dream by assimilating and, even when they were swayed by Zionist propaganda, were more likely to turn to the gradualists of the mainstream Zionists rather than the more fiery but still minority Revisionists. While Jabotinsky wanted to create a big army to defend the 'imminent' *Judenstaat*, the mainstream gradualists believed in the 'one more cow, one more *dunam*' approach to the development of their future country. The gradualists even tended to avoid the word 'statehood' as the *shem HaMephorash* (שם המפורש) ancient Hebrew for the unmentionable name of Jehovah. If they whispered the word 'state', then a state army was even more *sotto voce*.

Although British military intelligence developed specific small German-speaking Jewish units and a bigger commando group, they were reluctant to create a large army in case it became the tool for a major rebellion against British rule in Palestine. It was not until August 1944 that Churchill finally agreed to the creation of a 'Jewish Brigade'. The prime minister may been swayed by the intelligence he was getting about the extent of the Holocaust but it was probably more likely that he was trying to impress American public opinion.[3] When Churchill visited Washington on 18 May 1943 he opened his morning papers to read in the *New York Times* a full-page Zionist Organisation of America advert headlined: 'Churchill: drop the Mandate.' British departure from Palestine was inconceivable *then* though it was to come within five years. In the spring of the previous year worried British officials in the British embassy in Washington DC were counting the militant Zionist ads that were appearing in the US newspapers and reporting back to Foreign Minister Anthony Eden in London.

The need to rescue Jews in Europe had become a major electoral issue in the 1944 presidential campaign in the US and when President Roosevelt mentioned the need to balance good relations with Arab counties, Churchill told him that 'there were more Jews than Arab votes in the Anglo-Saxon countries and we could not afford to ignore such practical considerations'.[4]

The German Department

Before Erwin Rommel got anywhere near fulfilling his plan of smashing through Egypt and then conquering the whole of British Palestine, a special unit of German-speaking troops in Wehrmacht uniforms was active. This was during the so-called '200 days of anxiety' when it looked as though the Nazi armies were unstoppable. The Germans came close to destroying the British forces in Egypt and then sweeping up to Palestine. Rommel's near-victory is vividly exposed in Ken Delve's book, *Disaster in the Desert* – a clever 'alternative history'.[5]

The 'German Department' of the Jewish *Palmach* self-defence force was tasked, with British help, to set up a covert sabotage group called (inter alia) the 'Jewish Platoon' to work against a feared Nazi occupation. The commander of the Jewish platoon was Shimon Koch who, then aged 22, had migrated from Germany to Palestine in 1934. He renamed himself Shimon Avidan and later became a commander of the Givati Brigade during what the Israelis call their 'War of Independence'.

The *Palmach* (it means 'strike force') was an elite section of the Haganah. This was the main paramilitary organisation of the Jewish population (referred to locally as the Yishuv) in Mandate Palestine between 1920 and 1948, when it became the core of the Israel Defence Forces.

Hitler's armies had stormed across Europe and then Rommel's *Deutsches Afrikakorps* (later the *Panzerarmee Afrika* of Italian and German forces) rampaged in North Africa – with many Arabs cheering him on, especially those under European imperial rule. As the Jewish Platoon commander, Shimon Koch, put it, 'The Jewish community in the country was scattered at that time on small islands in a stormy Arabian sea … . It seemed that no power could stop Rommel from conquering the Land of Israel.' If the Germans invaded, the Haganah leaders decided that the entire Jewish population would be concentrated in the Carmel area, the north-western coastal part of the mandate. They decided that, if necessary, they would fight to the death as happened in Masada, when Jewish fighters were besieged by the Roman army in 73–4 CE. Then the starving survivors committed mass suicide rather than surrender.

That was the modern doomsday plan but meanwhile some young Jewish men volunteered to fight in various units of the British Army while others focused on their own efforts via the Haganah and *Palmach*. A few later decided to fight *against* the British but the vast majority preferred to work alongside the British forces. The German-speaking platoon was just one way of fighting back. Much of the platoon's ethos centred around a cave in the Mishmar Ha'emek forest, in the western Jezreel valley, adjacent to Mishmar Ha'emek kibbutz (which was founded in 1926 during the Third *Aliyah*, or wave, of immigrants, mainly from Poland). The kibbutz was at the centre of fighting during the Arab Revolt of 1936–39 and played a significant role during the War of Independence.

Britain's Royal Engineers trained Jewish volunteers specially in sabotage and wireless operation. Several tons of explosives were hidden in caches should the region come under German occupation. The cave in the forest became a symbol of resistance. It was full of German flags and books on the German army, mainly in German, as platoon members had to be native speakers of the language of the 'master race'. They searched for Aryan-looking Jews, where possible, preferably with blond hair and blue eyes. They sang German military songs and listened to German stations on a radio in the cave. They trained on captured German weapons and had to salute with an enthusiastic 'Heil Hitler'. They operated in various places around Palestine (although not in their German uniforms), including forming a maritime component. The 160 Palestinian Jews in the unit were assisted by British NCOs and officers.

The *Palmach*'s ethical code was encouraged in this secret unit, with commanders leading from the front and never abandoning an injured soldier; these became key elements of the Israel Defence Forces' code later. The secret unit specialised in creating a pseudo-German force but it also did covert training for a pseudo-Arab force, which, much later, was updated and dramatized in the *Fauda* TV series.

Shimon Koch was succeeded by Yehuda Ben Horin as commander of the German-speaking unit. Both men had been militant left-wingers from Silesia but had embraced the Zionist cause. German-speaking members of the troop had originally been envisaged not only as a stay-behind pseudo group in Palestine but also for special individual missions to parachute into occupied Europe. The unit did not fight as a single formation but did see action towards the end of the war. Some of the other Hungarian and Balkan secret British units were more often parachuted into Nazi-controlled Europe in 1944.

The *Palmach* worked with the British to create secret wireless stations throughout Palestine in case the British forces had to withdraw. While the Jewish platoon would act as a pseudo-German force, other *Palmach* commandos had co-operated with the British in drawing up a plan for the demolition of road and rail communications as well as industrial plants in a comprehensive scorched-earth policy.

It was not their regular British trainers who approached the German platoon and asked for volunteers one day in early 1942. Three British Army officers, from military intelligence in Cairo, requested volunteers to join a secret unit that became the Special Interrogation Group (SIG), initially tasked with mingling with German PoWs to gain intelligence. Albert Paz, a member of the German platoon, from Munich originally, volunteered. He recalled later: 'They took our measurements and prepared British military uniforms and notebooks for us. We were sent back home and told to tell nobody about our future mission.' Only three men finally volunteered (or were *allowed* by the *Palmach* to volunteer) for service in North Africa. Nevertheless, this was the nucleus of the secret British unit called the SIG. It was soon to fight hard against the German war machine in North Africa.

Chapter Two

The Special Interrogation Group

Origins

The idea came from a dashing young captain in the British Army called Herbert Cecil A. Buck MC. He'd had an adventurous career in the Raj where he was born in 1916 and initially joined 1st Battalion The Worcestershire Regiment in 1939, although his parent unit was 3rd/1st Punjab Regiment of the Indian Army. He was then selected for the SAS in 1942. He was also an Oxford scholar (St Peter's College), a fencing blue and fluent German-speaker. The German, if not the fencing, proved useful when he escaped from the *Afrikakorps* as a fugitive prisoner of war wearing a rough equivalent of a German uniform, including a real German forage cap. Buck had been commanding a company in the Punjab Regiment when he had been captured by the Germans at Gazala in January 1942. The *Afrikakorps* men had been using captured British vehicles which had helped to fool the Punjabi soldiers. The prisoners were not handled with customary Teutonic rigour, however, so Buck and others escaped from the temporary Libyan PoW cage. His fluent German enabled him to walk, and bluff, his way back to the British lines.

Buck was decorated with an MC for his escape. The official citation read:

Captain BUCK was captured South of DERNA on 2.2.42 and consistently tried in vain during the first forty eight hours to escape with some of his men before he was separated from them.

On 4.2.42 he planned to escape from BAROE with a Sergeant, but was moved to BENGHAZI. They arrived at 1700 hours and by

2000 hours were ready again, but the necessarily hasty reconnaissance caused them to mistake a sentry-box for an extra sentry and they postponed the attempt till next day. Unfortunately everyone was being moved to TRIPOLI, so Captain BUCK feigned sickness and avoided the move. That evening, the 5th February, Lt. MCKEE was brought in and they decided to escape together.

The P/W camp had been used for interning Italian civilians. After a further quick reconnaissance they chose the most feasible of two excellent escape plans. They slipped into an enemy shed with a window blown in, overlooking the wire and having timed the sentry beat, escaped through the wire in two to three minutes.

They worked their way through the hills and crossed the BARCE plain on the night of the 11th February to a position on the main road in the wooded hilly country West of TECNIS.

Here they waited till a suitable vehicle came by – a Ford 15 cwt. truck. Capt. BUCK, who speaks German, in a waterproof, leather jerkin and a cap resembling a German cap, stopped the driver, saw he was alone, so asked him for his pass in German and where he was going, then held him up with a spanner held to look like a revolver. Lt. MCKEE came up with a rifle and they bound and gagged the driver and left him behind in a bush. They decided to go via the desert driving through LAMLUDA where there had been a petrol point. While scouting for petrol at LAMLUDA they were seen, but escaped into the scrub followed by pistol shots although they lost their lorry.

The wandered about on foot from 12.2.42 till 20.2.42 and were joined by two officers of the Norfolk Yeomanry, a Sergeant and four O.R.'s of the Welch Regiment and a Flight Sergeant of the R.A.F.

On 20.2.42 they arrived on the main DERNA-TMIMI road about three miles West of UMM ER RZEM and 400 yards East of a German camp. After careful reconnaissance of the German troops in the district, with a German rifle over his shoulder, a British great-coat and jerkin and his German cap, Capt. BUCK stopped first a large staff car, but considered it unsuitable for his purpose, then at

2000 hours a German lorry. He asked the driver how many people he had (to ascertain if there were troops in the back). He replied two (they were seated in front) so Capt. BUCK said 'Hande hoch', the cue for Lt. MCKEE and another to come up on either side with pistols. While a third drove the truck down the road to where the remainder of the party were waiting and checked its petrol, oil and water, Capt. BUCK and Lt. MCKEE gagged the two Germans. They then climbed into the front of the lorry, wearing the Germans' caps.

Within five minutes they were on their way and, after driving by devious routes, reached British lines about eight miles West of ACROMA at dawn on February 21st.

Captain BUCK's escape is remarkable as an example of gallant, consistent and ingenious efforts to get away in spite of tremendous odds, supported by some extraordinarily quick thinking. He showed unselfishness in not escaping immediately after capture, but preferring to wait and help others. His powers of leadership in this direction were amply displayed where he afterwards led his little band of escapers back so gallantly to British territory. His courage, skill and initiative was mainly responsible for the escape of three other officers and six O.Rs.

Buck then persuaded the Special Operations Executive and Military Intelligence in Cairo that a small platoon of German-speakers could infiltrate the *Afrikakorps*. Some in the top brass in Cairo and London rather admired the boldness while others dubbed it 'Bertie Buck's suicide squad'. A few regarded such subterfuge as un-British, especially as the recent attempt to assassinate or capture Rommel had failed. Eventually the Buck project was passed and Lieutenant David Russell of the Scots Guards, another German-speaker, was made second-in-command. With his slicked-back hair and luxuriant moustache, he looked like the archetypal adventurer. Russell was a reckless motorcyclist, inevitably earning himself the nickname of the 'Flying Scotsman'. Famous for his escapades at Eton and later at Cambridge, he went on to earn the MC in North Africa.

Both Buck and Russell were men of action but not natural killers. Russell would write home to his sister from North Africa, explaining his dislike of killing Germans at close quarters. Despite his high intelligence, the more impulsive, and also more withdrawn Buck tended to be rather gullible in his judgements about other warriors, while Russell was more cautious and calculating.

In March 1942 the HQ of Military Intelligence in the War office in London agreed to the Buck project and Brigadier (later Lieutenant General) Terence Airey from the G (R) branch took over. He was a director of special operations and then Director of Military Intelligence in Cairo. He later became famous for his part in Operation FRITZEL (the name of the dachshund he was supposed to be buying in Switzerland). Actually, he was part of an Anglo-American deal (Operation SUNRISE) to persuade SS General Karl Wolff to end the war in Italy. Airey, an aristocratic officer with an aquiline nose and the deep penetrating blue eyes not uncommon in special forces' killers, loved cloak-and-dagger operations, Hence, his keenness to support the dashing Buck. Airey wrote the following order:

> A Special German Group as a sub-unit of the Middle East Commando – with the cover name of Special Interrogation Group – was to be used for infiltration behind the German lines in the Western Desert, under the 8th Army …. The strength would be approximately that of a platoon … . The personnel are fluent German linguists … mainly Palestinians (Jews) of German origin. Many of them have had war experience with 51 Commando.

London told Army HQ in Cairo to provide transport: 'one German Staff car and two 15 cwt Trucks'. The SIG received captured German weapons. They were also provided with paperwork for back-up stories and female Auxiliary Territorial Service (ATS) office workers in Army HQ in Cairo posed for pictures with SIG soldiers and copied love letters in German – all the paraphernalia of imagined lives back in the Third Reich. Sometimes staged Berlin backgrounds were used for photographs and often the ATS girls were chosen if they were blonde and looked suitably Aryan. Children were often invented and what the 'WAGs' did for the German war effort was endlessly rehearsed. Sometimes the SIG men chose a real person whom they knew so as to help with the consistency of the cover story. One Berliner had a sense of deadly irony: he selected the name of a pretty neighbour who was an ardent Nazi. The documents were produced on German army typewriters. They were also supplied with German cigarettes and German army paybooks as well as captured uniforms.

The desert war inspired a number of special forces. David Stirling's Special Air Service (SAS) and the Long Range Desert Group (LRDG) are the most well-known. Prime Minister Churchill had a passion for unconventional warfare. After the fall of Singapore and Tobruk, it was a chance, he believed, for the British to show the Yanks and Russians that they were fighting back. Another of the SF raiding forces was Popski's Private Army (No. 1 Demolition Squadron, PPA), set up in October 1942 and led by Major Vladimir Peniakoff. It was designed to disrupt Rommel's fuel supplies. As an Arabic speaker, Peniakoff had already established a small group called the Libyan Arab Force Commando (LAFC). Popski's unit, comprised initially of about twenty-three men, was unusual in that all officers reverted to the rank of lieutenant on joining and all other ranks reverted to privates. No bull (including drills and saluting) was tolerated and all the men messed together. The unit was moved to fight in Italy and was disbanded in 1945.

If Popski used indigenous Libyan Arabs, often with a profound dislike of the Italian colonisers, the Special Interrogation Group was made up of Jews who hated the Germans. Technically, the SIG was a sub-group of D Squadron of 1st Special Service Regiment, although it later worked closely with the LRDG and SAS. Captain Herbert Buck, as SIG commander, had visited the so-called 'German Platoon' in Palestine and recruited a handful of German-speaking volunteers from the *Palmach*, the strike force of the Haganah, the Jewish underground army. This was done with the full agreement of the military authorities in the Mandate.

He also met a young German-speaking Jewish girl in Palestine; Buck gave her a lift when she was hitchhiking with a girl-friend. This very young and impressionable girl happened to be Leah Schlossberg. Fascinated by the charming and erudite English officer, Leah invited Buck to meet the family in Tel Aviv and enjoy some German food. Leah went on to marry an Israeli general and future prime minister, Yitzhak Rabin.

Some of the Palestinian volunteers recruited by Buck, such as German-born Israel Carmi, had been active in the Special Night Squads pioneered by Orde Wingate and were later to join the Jewish Brigade and the Israel Defence Forces, a tribute to Wingate's original vision. Ariyeh Shai came from the British 51 Commando.

One SIG man was much older than the others. Karl Kahane, an Austrian, had served in the regular Austro-Hungarian army during the Great War and had been decorated. He was working as a town clerk in Austria and was forced to flee because of the *Anschluss.*

Maurice 'Monjo' Tiefenbrunner (also called 'Tiffen') was one of the main characters in the SIG – he is remembered for his bravery but also because he survived the war and wrote a short if powerful memoir, *A Long Journey Home.*

Most of the SIG troopers had fled Hitler, emigrated to Palestine and joined the British Army when war broke out. Tiefenbrunner did spend a short time in Palestine but he was not recruited from there by Buck. Born in Wiesbaden in 1915 to a very orthodox Jewish family, he was part of the so-called *OstJuden* community from Eastern Europe. His family ran a small *kosher* grocery shop. Tiefenbrunner did not attend a Jewish school and developed a taste for sport instead of the *Torah* (although he was also a member of Jewish sports clubs). His fitness was useful in later life and not just as a commando. In late 1934, when he was working in a small Jewish department store, Nazi thugs came in and assaulted Tiefenbrunner's boss; the future war hero defended his Jewish manager even though his heroics led to a few days in hospital. And now he was a marked man. Except that he had a sort of lucky break, one of many in his long adventurous life. All Jews of Polish background in Germany were forced to go back to Poland in 1938, and in October Tiefenbrunner's parents were arrested, imprisoned and taken to the local railway station to be deported to the east. One of the policemen at the station had been a pre-Nazi government schoolfriend and so Tiefenbrunner asked if he could take his mother's place so that she could return home to look after his younger siblings. Reluctantly, his old schoolfriend agreed. 'Reluctantly', because being kind to Jews, even if they had once been good friends, was not then very fashionable or even legal.[1]

Tiefenbrunner accompanied his blind father to Krakow where they stayed with relatives. A short time later he was called up for the Polish army. Tiefenbrunner spent a short unhappy period in Poland and, with some difficulty, then made his way to Antwerp, where his brother worked in the diamond-cutting business. Threatened with deportation, he was smuggled across the frontier to France.

With the help of local Irgun agents in Marseilles, he bribed his way onto a small pleasure craft that took him to an offshore cargo boat called *Parita*. Because it looked as if the Jewish passengers on the ship were going to be betrayed, a core of young Jewish men hijacked the ship with the support of the 850 aspiring inhabitants of a new Jewish homeland. They ran up the symbol that became the flag of Israel. After a total of seventy days at sea, many of the overcrowded passengers, especially the elderly, were ill and near starving. The crew members were bribed with all the valuables the refugees had and then most of the crew and officers were put in the lifeboats off the Palestinian coast while the small new Jewish crew, including Tiefenbrunner, ran the ship at full steam into the sands of Tel Aviv beach on 22 August 1939. There they smashed the engines to stop the British trying to re-launch the ship. The passengers were duly interned for one month and then released.

While in the internment camp, Tiefenbrunner naturally worried about his many relatives. Later he said: 'I was alone in Palestine, while my parents and a hundred other relatives were in dire straits in Poland. I had a dream that I could help them by joining the British Army and being parachuted into Poland.'

In Palestine, he did enlist in the British Army as a private in the Auxiliary Military Pioneer Corps (a year later restyled the Pioneer Corps) in December 1939 and was then sent to the UK. From Britain he was soon shipped with the unit to France. Two weeks after the French surrender he was evacuated from St Malo in one of the last ships to escape.

The young Tiefenbrunner's desire to fight the Nazis was not diminished. He joined 51 (Middle East) Commando and then fought in Eritrea against the Italians. Leading a section of machine gunners in the fierce battle of Keren, he was wounded and subsequently Mentioned in Despatches. The fighting around Keren in February-March 1941 involved mainly British and Indian troops plus Free French forces who were engaging with Axis troops for the first time since the fall of France. The bloody capture of Keren led to the collapse of Mussolini's position in the colony of Eritrea. A year later, in March 1942, Tiefenbrunner was asked to join the small and highly seret SIG.

The German-speaking SIG

Tiefenbrunner, along with many of his Jewish colleagues, assumed new names and/or also anglicised their old ones. The first training base for SIG was adjacent to the Geneifa PoW camp alongside the southern section of the Suez Canal just north of the town of Suez. Captain Buck had already recruited some Palestinian Jews lent by the *Palmach*. Other German-speaking Jews came from the Free Czech and Free French Forces. The cover name of the group has been debated; some historians have dubbed it the 'Special Intelligence Group' but the correct name is Special Interrogation Group. Also, the size of the special force has been debated. It was always slightly fewer than fifty members and the size varied according to, inter alia, casualties and temporary attachments elsewhere. Around 30,000 Palestinian Jews fought with the Allies, so this puts the small size of the elite SIG in perspective.

Another SIG member formerly in 51 Commando, Ariyeh Shai (he had other aliases), noted that their OC, Captain Buck, warned them right at the start 'that lives would depend on our ability to wear our disguises faultlessly, to learn to perfection the slang prevalent among the soldiers of the *Afrikakorps*, and to drill in accordance with all the

German methods. "If your true identity is found out," Buck said, "there is no hope for you.'"

They were kept in an isolated camp away from other British units and drilled endlessly in German. They were expected to 'Heil Hitler' with the utmost enthusiasm and sing bawdy soldiers' songs. Sometime during their training, they would be woken up in the early hours and they would be expected to reply immediately in German. Any Hebrew spoken and they would be expelled.

Isaac 'Harry' Levy, a Jewish chaplain of the Eighth Army, met some of the SIG troops by chance. Initially, he thought that they were prisoners of war. When the SIG men saw his Jewish chaplain insignia, they welcomed him and immediately shared their concerns that one of their number was not Jewish but was instead a German fifth-columnist who had spent time in Palestine. They asked the rabbi to pass on their fears to Buck. He did so but the OC was not convinced. His determination sometimes bordered on stubbornness, a not uncommon factor in special forces' soldiering.

Buck should have paid heed to the warnings from his men and the rabbi. There were indeed traitors in the midst of the SIG, supposedly one of the most secret units in the Allied forces. In November 1941 two members of the 361st Regiment of the *Afrikakorps* had been taken prisoner. They had both previously served in the French Foreign Legion: Feldwebel Walter Essner (also called Esser) and Unteroffozier Herbert/ Heinrich Brückner. Martin Sugarman, in his magisterial *Fighting Back*, quotes Tieffenbrunner's words: Brückner was 'big, brash and fair-haired in his twenties' while Essner 'was quiet and good-natured in his thirties'. They had been extensively questioned by the British Combined Services Detailed Interrogation Centre (CSDIC) in Egypt and eventually cleared to be double agents, initially picking up gossip in German PoW camps.

The British War Office ran a number of such centres around the world between 1942 and 1947, not just for the Middle East but for European countries and South Asia as well. They integrated uniformed military intelligence officers with, for example, operatives from MI5 and MI9. Originally, they concentrated on interrogating detainees, defectors and PoWs. According to Lieutenant Colonel G.L. Harrison, a former commanding officer of the CSDIC in Cairo, at least 40 per cent of British intelligence came from interrogation of PoWS, either as original data or secondary corroboration. From 1940–45 almost 500,000 Italian PoWs were held under British or Allied control. Nearly 316,000 were imprisoned directly by the British, who were adept at installing stool pigeons ('Z officers' in official parlance) in both the vast Italian camps and the smaller German ones. British military intelligence used both fluent Italian speakers and German speakers as professional Z officers who received extensive bonuses and privileges once out of the cages and camps. This is where some of the SIG troops were initially deployed. It was a psychologically demanding job: they had 'to maintain an air of genuineness and possess the versatility of an actor'.[2] Sometimes genuine prisoners could be turned to act as volunteer stool pigeons – this is where Brückner and Essner came in.

Some sources suggest that Brückner and Esser were sent from Cairo to Camp 020 at Latchmere House in south-west London. During the First World War, the sprawling Victorian mansion had been used as a hospital for soldiers with shell-shock. Then it was a central processing centre run by MI5 for turning German agents. It was run by Lieutenant Colonel Robin Stephens, nicknamed 'Tin Eye' because of the monocle he wore. Although Stephens was later tried for maltreatment of prisoners (including some deaths) when he was a commandant at a post-war camp for senior Nazis in Germany, he insisted that there would be no physical torture at Latchmere. His instructions to his interrogators were specific:

> Never strike a man. In the first place it is an act of cowardice. In the second place, it is not intelligent. A prisoner will lie to avoid further punishment and everything he says thereafter will be based on a false premise.

Colonel Stephens, half-German himself, kicked out a senior interrogator for over-harsh methods. It was no holiday camp, however, as 'Tin Eye' claimed that he could break a man in a few days. Ian Cobain, in his 2012 book, *Cruel Britannia*, claimed that inmates were regularly mistreated, including mock executions. Members of the British Union of Fascists were singled out for particularly brutal treatment. William Joyce, aka Lord Haw-Haw, was interrogated there before he was hanged for treason in 1946. Isolation and sleep deprivation were common tactics. Prisoners were often hooded for long periods. Inmates could not talk to each other and there were no cigarettes. The food was deliberately kept bland and sparse. Colonel Stephens, dressed in his uniform as a Gurkha officer, would often conduct extremely lengthy sessions himself, believing himself to be a natural 'breaker' of men. Some of his own officers feared him and thought him mad.

Latchmere had been opened in June 1940 and it became known to its inmates as Camp 020. It was also called The Cage, although smaller cages for interrogation existed throughout the UK. The ultimate control was exercised by MI9 and later, MI19, directorates of Military Intelligence in the War Office in London. The Americans were regular visitors and some of its trainers worked at The Cage. By 1943 it was agreed that American or British interrogators could work on the prisoners, regardless of their nationality. As the war progressed, the system spread to interrogation centres in Beirut, Algiers, Naples, Rome and even as far as the Red Fort in Delhi. Cairo was one of the busiest, however, especially during the desert war. The interrogators there began to experiment with amphetamines and thyroxine. One medical staff member, a former psychiatrist, prided himself on the use of hypnosis.

During the war, Camp 020, as it was usually called, achieved a great deal: probably the most famous was the Double Cross System. Nearly every Nazi agent who entered UK was caught and often turned (or executed). (There were a handful of exceptions – those who were not caught and understandably kept quiet after the war.) And, amusingly, the Germans kept sending money to the turned and fabricated agents and this more than paid for the costs of the whole Double Cross structure. The XX Committee that ran Double Cross recruited much of their personnel via Latchmere.

Despite their fancy methods, in retrospect it appears that Cairo and/or London slipped up with the two SIG ex-Wehrmacht men despite their lengthy interrogation. The fact that they had originally fought for France in the Foreign Legion added extra lustre to their claims to be anti-Hitler. Brückner was a pseudonym for Brockmann; the name Esser/Essner was probably also false. CSDIC regularly provided new identities for captured or surrendered enemy personnel who had agreed to act as double agents. For the sake of clarity, the names that are deployed most often will be used here.

Although both men were Germans, they professed to be virulently anti-Nazi. British military intelligence believed them, as did Captain Buck; Tiefenbrunner and others in the SIG did not. One of the SIG men privately described Buck as 'brilliant but naïve' partly because he shrugged off the complaints about the turncoats. And the SIG troopers were very reluctant to go into action with the two 'turned' soldiers though the supposedly anti-Nazi Germans had been very thorough in their job of drilling the SIG recruits in the ways of the Wehrmacht in general and *Afrikakorps* in particular.

Latchmere specialised in setting up German double agents in the UK. Sending back doctored intelligence by radio from England was one thing but the two former *Afrikakorps* sergeants were turned to infiltrate and kill their former brothers in arms. When they arrived at Buck's camp near the Bitter Lakes in May 1942, they had a clean bill of health but they had a lot to prove.

In their barracks, the SIG commandos were woken up by shouts of *Kompanie aufstehen!* They immediately endured a lengthy PT session before any breakfast. Except for meals and some restricted sleep their training included day and night exercises with German weapons and learning German marching songs. When they went to the mess for meals they were expected to goose-step there. Their intensive and skilled training by Brückner and Essner forged the Jewish troops into a tight replica of a Wehrmacht unit. Besides weapons handling, they underwent explosives training, desert navigation and unarmed combat. They also became expert drivers and mechanics on the captured German vehicles they trained on. Some of the men had been commandos in other British units while others, including some of the *Palmach* men, had been in the

Special Night Squads. They possessed excellent basic material to be fashioned into an elite SF unit.

Operations

Their initial forays behind enemy lines were intelligence gathering. The first was near Bardia, the former Italian-controlled port and fortress near the Egyptian border. In January 1941 Australian troops had captured this town that helped to collapse the Italian campaign that in turn led to Rommel's spectacular intervention in North Africa. SIG commandos, posing as German military police, now set up roadblocks in the reconquered territory and questioned German transport convoys. Their data on troop movement proved very useful. Sometimes they would pull into German camps and just gossip with unsuspecting *Afrikakorps* members and gather useful information. They occasionally inflicted minor acts of sabotage. On one occasion Tiffen, as Tiefenbrunner now preferred to be called, queued up to draw pay from a Wehrmacht field cashier. Afterwards he explained in his quiet voice that, although he was nervous, he was so busy living his assumed role that he did not have time to stop and consider how dangerous this action was. The SIG men also continued their occasional intelligence gathering with Germans in British PoW camps.

All this was a tactical preamble to SIG's participation in a major strategic action. Malta was vital to the British control of the Mediterranean; that is why it endured three years of naval siege and endless attacks by the Italian and German air forces. The island-fortress was a central component in interdicting the supply lines to Rommel's forces in North Africa. If Allied forces could disrupt the aerial assaults on British shipping lanes as well as the Malta garrison, then the *Afrikakorps* could be denied supplies from Europe. Two British convoys, one from Gibraltar and another from Alexandria, were due to set sail in June 1942 to run the gauntlet to supply the near-starving military garrison and civilian population of Malta. Churchill had called Malta an unsinkable aircraft carrier, although the Royal Navy had considered it almost *indefensible* because of its closeness to Italy. That is why the navy shifted its Mediterranean HQ to Alexandria in

1939. Rommel had immediately recognised its importance. In May 1941 he said presciently, 'Without Malta, the Axis will end up losing control of North Africa.' It was vital as it was the only British base between Gibraltar and Alexandria. At the beginning of 1942 there was a series of convoys that tried to run the Axis blockade of Malta which had come under sustained Axis attack by sea and air. At one stage exhausted and half-starved RAF ground crews could manage to maintain just a handful of serviceable fighter aircraft.[3]

Seven German airfields in North Africa were identified by British intelligence as key targets to stop the southern bases of air attack in the Malta campaign. This is where the SIG unit came in. They were tasked with helping the SAS commander, then Major David Stirling, with his mission to blow up aircraft at Derna and Martuba, two German airfields about 100 miles west of Tobruk. Stirling had approached Buck who was more than delighted to help. The SIG component was to meet the SAS at Siwa oasis in early June 1942. Although the survivors' accounts and the official records disagree slightly in the details of personnel and vehicles deployed, a small convoy of German and 'captured' British vehicles set out on the night of on 6 June. Tiffen said that there were twelve SIG commandos in all (although that number seems rather high). There was also a small group of Free French troops and SAS. The SIG men were to don their German uniforms and pose as guards for the 'captured' French troops whose weapons were hidden in the trucks. A New Zealand component of the Long Range Desert Group went ahead to set up an RV and wait for the SIG unit to return.

After four days, the SIG commandos donned their Wehrmacht disguise. Captain Buck was dressed as an *Afrikakorps* private driving the command car. Next to him were the suspect SIG Germans, Brückner and Essner, dressed as NCOs, their real former ranks. Atop each truck, German-style, was a SIG man. The Jewish commandos each carried a Luger, machine gun, a killing knife and grenades. Besides the French soldiers' concealed arms, two ready-mounted machine guns were hidden.

The first difficulty was not German military efficiency but the more relaxed Italian sense of security and even hospitality. In a late and very hot Libyan afternoon, around 4.00 pm, a very skinny Italian soldier demanded the June password at a roadblock with a small guardroom. Buck knew the May one but military intelligence had not updated him. The Italian guard would not budge when the 'Germans' explained that they had been in the desert and had not been updated with the latest password. Buck waved their forged papers. Then a well-dressed Italian major arrived and genially suggested they discuss the matter over a glass of wine in the relative coolness of his office.

Brückner and Buck joined the major for an affable chat and a glass of wine. The Italian officer would not relent, however, despite his charm and good manners. Then Buck gave the nod to Brückner and the German launched into an abusive Teutonic rant in his native tongue. 'I'll report you to my superiors … . Don't you see that German soldiers are coming back from a tough trip in the desert?' That a German NCO could speak to a major in that tone demonstrates the Italian subservience to the master race. The major gave way.

The intruders soon reached another roadblock, this time a German one. But the chubby Wehrmacht corporal soon waved the bogus convoy through – with a warning that British commandos were operating in the area. They stopped on the edge of a German camp and filled up with fuel and bought some provisions. One of their team, Ariyeh Shai, even queued up for some supper in the mess – lentils and dumplings. He'd long had a craving for real German food. Shortly afterwards they parked a few miles down the road.

The next day, 13 June 1942, the phantom force decided to recce the two Derna airfields. Brückner drove, accompanied by a Free French officer and four other men. The one airfield boasted Messerschmitt 110 fighter-bombers, while they saw Stukas at the other air base. They did not push their luck by trying to recce the Martuba airfields as well. That night the marauders split their force to hit the two groups of airfields simultaneously. Meanwhile, two SIG men had managed to get the correct password for June ('siesta' and the reply was 'Eldorado').

Buck, with Essner, led one party to hit Martuba. The second group with Brückner stopped the team near the cinema in the town of Derna.

On the pretence that the engine was overheating, he said he needed to go to a garage but instead he ran to a nearby German guardroom. The betrayal that followed has inspired several versions but in essence the Free French in the main wagon saw that they were surrounded by German soldiers with guns at the ready. 'All Frenchmen get out,' the Germans ordered. The commandos came out with guns blazing. Many *Afrikakorps* soldiers were killed or wounded before the Free French troops were nearly all killed or captured. Two SIG men, Eliyahu Gottlieb and Peter Haas, were cornered. Knowing only too well what their fate would be if they were captured, they fought to the death: they blew themselves up with their own grenades. The French commander, Lieutenant Augustine Jordain, manged to escape in the melee and then reach the RV, despite his wounds.

Buck's raid at Martuba, however, had succeeded in destroying twenty planes. Brückner had betrayed the RV as well. The Germans hit the surviving SIG, SAS and French commando team. With one lorry, the survivors made their way to Siwa oasis. Then they waited for stragglers for almost a week at Baltel Zalegh. But none came. Meanwhile, they also managed to persuade a German spotter plane to hold its fire by laying out a large swastika flag in the sand.

At the strategic level, Malta had been relieved by a diminished convoy from Gibraltar, while the second battered convoy had to turn around to limp back to Alexandria. At the tactical level, some of the SIG men, one Frenchman and some SAS troopers, managed to get home with the help of the LRDG. Brückner was flown to Germany and, in one version, was personally decorated with the *Deutsche Kreuz* by the Führer himself.[4]

Tiffen closely guarded Essner all the way back to Cairo, where he was allegedly shot while trying to escape. Actually, a chastened Buck had ordered two of his men to shoot him in the desert. The SIG unit lived to fight again – in a much bigger operation: a major raid on Tobruk. The refugees turned avengers would go down in Jewish history as 'Lions of Judah'.

They needed to be lions because, after the Brückner betrayal, British intelligence intercepted this signal to the *Afrikakorps* on 13 June 1942:

Most Secret document – only to be opened by an officer – from Supreme Commander of the Army to Panzer Army Africa – there are said to be numerous German political refugees with Free French forces in Africa. The Führer has ordered that the severest measures are to be taken against those concerned. They are therefore to be immediately wiped out in battle and in cases where they escape being killed in battle, a military sentence is to be pronounced immediately by the nearest German officer and they are to be shot out of hand, unless they have to be temporarily retained for intelligence purposes. This order is NOT to be forwarded in writing: commanding officers are to be told verbally.

Hitler knew that his order constituted a war crime, hence the reluctance to commit the order to paper.

Chapter Three

The Raid on Tobruk

Desert warfare

The Special Interrogation Group were to meet their Armageddon in this raid. It would make their secret reputation secure but Operation AGREEMENT would also mean the end of the unit although some of the SIG troops would fight on in other special forces.

The fighting in the deserts of North Africa was unlike the other theatres of the Second World War. Except for the special forces' operations in the deep desert, the main campaigning was largely limited to the coastal plains. (During the 1941 CRUSADER offensive, however, a deep thrust was made by Force E as part of the overall Eighth Army plan. Commanded by Brigadier Denys Reid, Force E was also known as Oasis Force and seized most of the southern oases.) With the sea on one side and, on the other, scrub and desert usually hemmed in by high ground or steep depressions, the space to fight was generally not more than about forty miles wide – but this potential combat zone extended for 1,200 miles, stretching from the Libyan capital of Tripoli in the west to Alexandria in Egypt to the east. Although the terrain often offered exuberant opportunities for highly mobile tank warfare, which suited the *Afrikakorps*, supply was a constant problem as there was nothing to forage in the vast empty deserts. Therefore, each port represented a logistical solution and so the see-saw war often inspired swift advances and reverses between coastal objectives. With the exception of the sieges of Tobruk and El Alamein, the desert war was extremely mobile and fluid. Erwin Rommel had the advantage in that he believed in speed rather than any acquisition of territory. Often chronically short of fuel, water and reinforcements, Rommel had to rely on his genius at mobility to outmanoeuvre his enemies. In the end, logistics defeated Rommel despite his skills in mobile armoured warfare.

Rommel was always an outsider, partly because he spoke with a pronounced southern German or Swabian accent unlike the Prussian aristocracy who dominated the Wehrmacht high command. Also, Rommel felt that he should be physically and morally more robust than the troops he commanded, so he always tried to set a tough and aggressive example and expected his senior commanders to do the same. Rommel believed that leading from the front was vital but he often took it too far. He frequently directed a single company or battalion and so made communication with his HQ difficult – they never knew where he was and it also risked his life – not least being killed by his own artillery let alone by the enemy. Some of his admirers knew that they could not restrain their boss in the field but they thought that his self-destructive Spartan personal life-style as well as his style of command diminished his strategic effectiveness. His support staff had to try to 'baby' him as unobtrusively as possible.

Rommel possessed a ferocious and boundless energy as well as great personal courage. But he tended to ignore administrative problems and fought like an eighteenth-century general rather than one from the twentieth century. During the advance in April 1941, for example, he led in person from the front in numerous local attacks and was everywhere in the battles except at his own headquarters. His staff officers were often as surprised by his movements as his opponents.

Nevertheless, Rommel gained a tremendous reputation – on both sides of the war. The German general was a military genius but the idea that he fought a 'war without hate' was a myth. An *Afrikakorps* officer liaised closely with the SS units that robbed and murdered North African Jews, leading to the so-called 'Mystery of Rommel's gold' that was never found. Perhaps it never existed, despite the extensive Jewish spoils seized by the Nazis. The Jews who fought for Britain against Rommel never swallowed the myth: they knew that they would be murdered if caught. Nevertheless, many in Eighth Army lionised the Desert Fox – to mix metaphors. So much so that Allied intelligence tried hard to undermine Rommel's popular myth, to little avail because he so often outfought the Allies, while the Allied generals kept losing – until finally Eighth Army had an overwhelming superiority in tanks, aircraft, manpower and logistics. A popular joke at the time had Hitler secretly contacting Churchill with an offer to remove Rommel from his command in exchange for Churchill *retaining all* his generals in exactly the same positions.

General Sir Claude Auchinleck warned his officers that:

they should not let the men turn Rommel into a bogey man for our troops, because they talk about him so much. He is not superhuman, energetic and capable as he is. And even if were superhuman, it would be most undesirable for our soldiers to attribute supernatural powers to him.

*   *   *

Few accurate maps had been made of the desert wastes up until the Second World War. When the famous Long Range Desert Group was formed in 1940 its commanders could find only one small-scale Libyan map in the whole of Cairo and that map was dated 1915; even this contained little more information than the standard Friedrich Rohlfs map of 1874. Perhaps the lack of mapping was due to the fact that only one tarmac road existed in the whole of Libya and that ran mostly along the coast or in places within fifty miles of the Mediterranean. This route extended from Tunis to Alexandria. Some of the better-known desert tracks inland were sometimes marked out by tall iron beacons or, later, by empty oil drums. The desert special forces had to navigate as if at sea, relying on the sun, the stars and a compass. The Long Range Desert Group demonstrated some old lore of special force operations: detailed planning, first-class equipment, reliable and simple communications and excellent troops.

The Libyan desert was roughly the same size as British India: immense and, to the untrained eye, almost featureless. But the experienced desert travellers soon got to recognise perhaps a pile of stones or the long-dried carcass of a camel. These could stand out for miles on the wide-open horizon. And the fact that some dunes could reach a height of six hundred feet also marked out routes although the dunes could shift.

Water was inevitably the dominant ingredient of desert survival. Along the coast, rainfall generated some vegetation but in the deep south there was none except for the occasional oases. In some places in southern Libya it may not have rained for decades. The large area of sand seas was considered impassable for any form of motor vehicle, although intrepid explorers did navigate between and around the sand seas before the outbreak of war in 1939. The desert warriors of the Second World War had to contend with extreme temperatures of intense searing heat by day and yet freezing temperatures at night.

The balance of forces

In the summer of 1940 British ground forces in Egypt numbered around 36,000 troops. Britain had lost its chief imperial ally in the region, though some of the French colonial forces were anti-Vichy. France had been defeated at home and it looked as though the Nazis were about to follow the conquest of France with the invasion of Britain in Operation SEALION. It was an opportune time for the Italian imperial forces in Libya and the Horn of Africa to move against the isolated government in London as it stood alone, without any formal alliance with the Americans. The small British infantry forces in Egypt were backed by over 200 land-based aircraft and over 300 armoured cars and tanks in the well-trained 7th Armoured Division. General Sir Archibald Wavell was the commander in chief in the Middle East (which included Greece, the Balkans and East Africa, not to forget Palestine and Syria). Wavell had also overseen the defeat of the Italians in the East African campaign, liberating Abyssinia in the first British victory of the war. That campaign included Wingate and was commanded by Alan Cunningham who became the first commander Eighth Army in October 1941.

Wavell's main job, however, was protecting the vital artery of the Suez Canal against Rome's plans to send in an invasion force to take Cairo. The Italians had ten times more men than the British, although they were generally poorly equipped and led. Wavell has tended to get a bad press for his Middle East command once Rommel came on the scene, but he did smash the initial Italian invasion and captured 130,000 prisoners as well as 400 tanks in what was probably the greatest British Commonwealth's victory of the war. That Italian defeat, however, led to the entry of an entirely different calibre of fighting men: the *Afrikakorps* under Erwin Rommel.

Young Wavell's headmaster had originally advised Wavell's father (also a general) that there was no need to send him into the army as he had 'sufficient ability to make his way in other walks of life'. Wavell then spent nearly his whole career in the army reaching the rank of Field Marshal. Rommel rated him but Churchill did not and so Wavell was eventually replaced by General Sir Claude Auchinleck, known universally as the 'Auk'.

Some historians would argue that the Germans out-thought and out-fought the British military leadership (although Auchinleck defeated Rommel in Operation CRUSADER and did so again at Alamein). Nevertheless, one of the most crushing defeats for the Allies was the capitulation of the Tobruk garrison in June 1942; this came only four months after a similar debacle in the fall of Singapore, the largest surrender of British forces in history. Prime Minister Churchill was in Washington meeting President Franklin D. Roosevelt when he heard the news of the Tobruk catastrophe. Churchill later wrote:

> I did not attempt to hide from the President the shock I received. It was a bitter moment. Defeat is one thing: disgrace is another.

Rommel, bolstered by the booty captured in Tobruk, pushed on, intending to capture the whole of Egypt and especially the vital Suez artery. It was not just about the canal. If Egypt had fallen, the hinge of three continents would have snapped. Eighty per cent of transport in the *Panzerarmee Afrika* was now captured British vehicles. The Germans pushed on deep into Egypt before being halted at El Alamein, where the British Eighth Army made its last stand. Churchill described them as 'brave but baffled'. The Auk tried to suppress the general atmosphere of defeatism. Even the British Mediterranean Fleet left Alexandria while panic started to overwhelm Cairo, and the Arab nationalists and other pro-fascists jubilantly counted the days until total Allied surrender. US military intelligence predicted on 30 June that Rommel would be in Cairo in a week.

One of Churchill's favourites was Fitzroy Maclean, daring commando, and later a politician, and considered to be part of the model for Ian Fleming's James Bond. Maclean wrote in his acclaimed book, *Eastern Approaches*, that

> In Cairo, the staff at HQ Middle East were burning their files and the Italian colony were getting out their black shirts and fascist badges in preparation for Mussolini's triumphant entry.

It was in this depressing context that Operation AGREEMENT emerged. A small raid was transformed into a big plan to save the Allies' reputation in the North African war. Pious hopes and delusional ambitions were fed by desperation and frustration.

Rommel, however, had outrun his lines of communication. Because the invasion of Russia was to forestall any major reinforcement, the first battle of El Alamein was to mark the high-water mark of the amazing German advance, even though it seemed to many at the time (though not Auchinleck) that the Nazi push into the Nile Delta was almost inevitable. Rommel had got so close to his goal. 'I could weep,' he confided in his diary. The Germans were now on the defensive: they were finally being outfought by Auchinleck, as the German field marshal also confided in his diary.

The Auk, for his part, was confiding in his diary and then openly advocating, the return of the death penalty for cowardice and desertion on the field of battle. This was not the first time that a Second World War commander had asked for a practice that had been used in the Great War. But the stories of those 'shot at dawn' had been extremely unpopular with the public and the Labour government had abolished military firing squads in 1930. When the measure was brought before the War Cabinet Churchill was opposed, as were the Labour members of the wartime coalition. The request revealed, however, the often poor state of morale in Eighth Army in the spring and summer of 1942.

Operation AGREEMENT

This was the context for the big raid on Tobruk by a Britain that was desperate to turn the fortunes of war with a bold surprise attack. The main thrust, called Operation AGREEMENT, was centred on a ground and amphibious attack in mid-September 1942 on Axis-held Tobruk. The plan was to destroy nearby airfields, harbour facilities and defences and large oil stores as well as free and arm thousands of Allied PoWs. At the same time diversionary attacks were made on Benghazi, the Gialo oasis and Barce.

The Battle Plan for Operation AGREEMENT

6 September
Force B to move out from Kufra Oasis and form up outside Tobruk defences

10 September
Midday Sudan Defence Force elements to march towards Bahariya Oasis in readiness for the attacks on Siwa – Operation COASTGUARD

13 September
Force A sails from Haifa aboard Tribal-class destroyers
Force C MTBs and launches sail from Alexandria.
21.30   Air raid on Tobruk begins
21.45   Force B secures its immediate objectives to prepare for Force
        C to land.

14 September
01.30   Allied bombers cease dropping flares.
01.40   HM Submarine *Taku* puts Folbot section in the water near
        Tobruk.

02.00   Folbots reach the shore and mark landing beach for Force A.

02.00   Force C enters the Mersa Umm Es Sciause cove, provided the right signals are given.

02.30   Force C comes ashore in the inlet.

03.00   Destroyers arrive off the coast.

03.40   The two waves of marines come ashore.

03.40   Bombing ceases but RAF runs diversionary flights.

04.15   All air operations cease.

04.15   Force C MTBs and launches enter Tobruk harbour to attack shipping.

09.00   Destroyers enter the harbour

Force Z leaves Kufra to attack Gialo Oasis.

16 September

Force Z to have secured Gialo.

The amphibious force consisted mainly of around 400 Royal Marines and 180 Argyll and Sutherland Highlanders. The land elements had come north from the desert and were led by Lieutenant Colonel John Edward 'Jock' Haselden. He was a Lawrence of Arabia figure who was brought up in Egypt and spoke fluent Arabic and had often penetrated the enemy on foot dressed as an Arab. Also speaking fluent French and Italian, he was a fearless intelligence officer who had earned the MC and Bar. Colonel Haselden led a force that captured an Italian 152mm coastal battery but the landing force of supporting Marines and commandos had difficulty landing, partly due to bad sea conditions and the failure to set up beacons. The British Tribal-class destroyer HMS *Sikh*, which was supposed to lead the landing, was hit by Italian 152mm shore batteries and German 88mm anti-tank guns and anti-aircraft artillery. HMS *Zulu*, her sister ship, tried to tow her away as *Sikh* lost the ability to steer. *Zulu*, which had played a crucial role in destroying the *Bismarck*, sank later. HMS *Coventry* was so badly damaged that she had to be scuttled. The smaller boats such as MTBs mostly failed to land or landed in the wrong place.

The Allies lost 800 killed and 576 captured while fifteen Italians and one German were killed. German troops, however, were crucial in stopping the Italians killing Haselden's captured men. Haselden himself was killed in action but some of his men had to eventually surrender: they had initially killed a number of Italians manning the shore battery. The Royal Navy lost one cruiser and two destroyers as well as four MTBs, plus some other small landing craft.

Overall, the raid was a disaster but it was not totally so for the SIG, because the Jewish soldiers, called 'Palestinians' in contemporary military records, played a major role in actually getting into Tobruk. German-speaking Jewish volunteers from 51 Commando, as well as from the Special Interrogation Group, had been used individually to help in special ops. Two of the stars of the SAS firmament, Paddy Mayne and David Stirling, had deployed Karl Kahane, a SIG man in German uniform, to bluff their way through Axis roadblocks in the vicinity of Benghazi. Kahane unleashed a torrent of German abuse at a sentry who had been rash enough to challenge the SAS. Another German Jewish volunteer had been a member of the ill-starred Operation FLIPPER to kill or capture Rommel in November 1941. The ever-active Jock Haselden had done the recce but Rommel had moved his HQ some time before and was, anyway, in Rome at the time of the attack. (Some German historians claim that no plot to assassinate Rommel had ever occurred in North Africa, although there were others in 1944.) Rommel himself was bemused because the targeted HQ in Libya was 250 miles behind the front line and the charismatic German warrior was known for always being in the front line with his men.[1]

The ever-resourceful Haselden was leading the land force in Operation AGREEMENT, which included Captain Buck and five SIG men. Following the previous betrayal by Brückner, Buck was much more cautious now, not least because the ruse obviously might not work a second time; originally twelve SIG troops were supposed to join the Tobruk assault. The LRDG led the force (Force B) from Kufra Oasis. The SIG men plus eighty-three commandos rode in eight 3-ton Chevrolet trucks. The LRDG were to remain in the desert outskirts, while the SIG men were to bluff their way through the Tobruk perimeter posing as German guards for the 'captured' Brits – the commandos. The commandos were tasked to first capture the coastal guns at Mersa Umm es Sciause, east of the harbour.

Buck also had a plan to capture a German general whose location British intelligence had discovered. The marauders were supposed to release, and help arm, many of the thousands of British PoWs in Tobruk. All this was to be done after assisting the amphibious assault and then escaping back into the desert, although many of the commandos were supposed to get off in the destroyers.

That was the original – very over-ambitious – plan.

The SIG men had been flown to the airfield at Kufra Oasis in an RAF Bristol Bombay transport/bomber. It could carry twenty-four armed men or ten stretchers as it was often deployed to evacuate wounded troops. The commandos already there were amazed to see the SIG men in German uniforms, conducting German drill and using German commands. Besides Buck they were, officially, Corporal Weizmann and Privates Wilenski, Hillman, Berg and Steiner but they would have used English aliases. Buck's second-in-command was Lieutenant David Russell, a Scots Guards officer who also spoke fluent German.[2] Because of the betrayal in the previous year, some of the LRDG men at Kufra were distrustful of the SIG men, who anyway kept to themselves. The LRDG warriors knew some of them were very brave but the fatal betrayal of the French special forces had obviously left a bitter legacy.

The commando convoy did not attract attention from the air because so many British vehicles were used by the Axis forces. The SIG men had used original German stencils to put identifications on the cab roofs to fool any over-curious Stuka pilots. They also painted a white stripe across the bonnets. This was a sign of captured booty or *Beutezeichen*. The SIG soldiers carried fake passes and current ID documents. After the LRDG escorts left, three trucks made for the main tarmac road leading to Tobruk. Buck sat in the front one dressed as a German officer; the other SIG men acted as German guards for the 'captured' commandos. When they reached the Tobruk perimeter fence they were waved through by Italian guards while the other SIG men threw half-friendly insults at their despised 'allies'.

One vehicle in the convoy had a minor glancing collision with a German staff car but the Brits didn't stop and then they were accompanied by two heavily-armed army motorcycles with sidecars. After what seemed ages, the motorbikes overtook the convoy and went on their way. At about 9.00pm, in the darkness, Colonel Haselden noted the bombproof oil storage depot that was supposed to be destroyed later that night. All around the three-truck convoy, numerous tented encampments twinkled as Italians and Germans went about their duties, oblivious to the enemy within. Eventually, the intruders found a side turning off the main road. They were almost immediately met by a harsh challenge in German. One of the commando officers got out and walked into the darkness. He soon returned with a German rifle. A little further on, the commandos got out of the three lorries and put on full combat kit. Nearby were the buildings they were looking for, the administrative centre for the coast defences they were supposed to destroy.

At 10.30 pm on 13 September 1942 the RAF started their bombing raid to soften up the port defences.

Haselden led some of the SIG team and his own commandos in capturing a small villa and killed, or put to flight, the Italian occupants. The colonel used this villa as his new HQ and organised various local attacks on machine-gun posts and a wireless station. At 2.00am Haselden – at the last minute – issued the codeword 'Nigger' for the amphibious forces to land. Because of heavy fire from coast guns and poor communications, only two of the sixteen MTBs managed to land with just a handful of reinforcements. By this time, realising that Tobruk was being hit by air, land and amphibious forces, German officers were fully engaged in organising themselves and their Italian allies to launch a full-scale defence.

The SIG men cleared several Italian positions and then moved inland, as planned, to act as a rearguard to resist any counter-attack from the direction of their departure from the tarmac road. They captured a number of anti-aircraft emplacements and held them despite Italian counter-attacks. They couldn't use the captured guns as they were very old and without sights and ammunition. Eventually, the SIG men rolled grenades into the ack-ack gun barrels to destroy them.

Due to the lack of reinforcements because of the general failure of the amphibious landings, Haselden's commandos were being worn down by constant fire. Buck ordered his men to get rid of their German documents and find British uniforms from dead commandos. Wilenski and Weizmann went off to destroy one lorry and Buck and Russell suddenly re-appeared as their plan to release PoWs had been aborted. Haselden ordered the surviving commandos to escape in the two remaining trucks. Despite the four hours of non-stop combat defending his temporary HQ, he was calm and totally in charge of himself and his fighters. Buck yelled at Steiner, however, to get rid of his German uniform, even though he himself was still dressed as an *Afrikakorps* officer.

The colonel was still fighting hard and led the way as Russell, Buck and the SIG men followed him. Berg was wounded as Haselden was killed by a grenade. Steiner managed to drag Berg away from the heavy Italian fire. The majority of the escapees were forced to surrender – they had no water, food or in most cases any ammo and some were carrying wounded comrades.

Only a handful of the group formerly led by Haselden escaped and managed the hard trek to British lines. Russell got back, as did the wounded Berg and Wilenski.[3] Weizmann was initially with the SIG survivors but he was wounded while foraging for food and after seventeen days insisted on being left behind so as not encumber his colleagues. Local Libyan Arabs captured him and handed him over to the Italians who in turn gave him to the Gestapo. After five days of torture, he revealed absolutely nothing. He was even put in front of a firing squad but an *Afrikakorps* officer eventually persuaded the Gestapo to release him into a PoW camp.

Private Steiner had joined the small group led by Lieutenant Tommy Langton (SBS/Irish Guards). Apparently, Steiner knew that the Germans had his name and aliases, so he asked his group to refer to him as 'Ken' Kennedy. He held up during the evasion due to his bravery and resourcefulness. During the escape he had lost his left boot and his foot was lacerated by barbed wire. As a fluent Arabic speaker from his time in Palestine, he managed to negotiate for food with the local Arab villages, as well as securing new boots. Steiner was not obviously a natural warrior; the short 19-year-old SIG private had been born the son of a Viennese butcher. The future SIG hero had been locked up at 16 for anti-Nazi activities. He managed to escape to Palestine where he joined the Pioneer Corps under the very brief illusion that they were a British fighting force. So he joined the tough 51 Middle East Commandos and fought in Eritrea as did Maurice Tiefenbrunner. Eventually, the SIG group reached Allied lines 400 miles east of Tobruk on 13 November. They had marched for two months, with Steiner initially walking with a bare foot. Steiner was nursed back to health in a South African-run convalescent centre.

This marked the end of the SIG as a discrete fighting force. The unit had a short life but the story included many epic adventures. Among themselves they sometimes referred to their missions as *himmelfahrts* – literally, trips to heaven.

They had played their role bravely in an operation that was terribly over-complicated although Jock Haselden's original plan had been basic and simple. As one historian noted, 'Lapses in security, lamentable and inexcusable as they were, did not determine failure or pre-doom the assault … . Even if all the landings had gone swimmingly, the men coming ashore would have been facing impossible odds.'[4]

Whether the enemy had been tipped off has been endlessly debated. Despite all the loose talk in Cairo and Alexandria, as well as the efficiency of Rommel's signals intelligence,[5] on balance the defenders in Tobruk were not specifically forewarned. The SAS Benghazi raid was definitely compromised by advance intelligence. The Barce raid worked because it had very limited objectives: get in fast and get out. And the fewer cogs the better. Spoiling raids seemed to work at this stage of the war, whereas Operation AGREEMENT had 'grown like Topsy'. General Bernard Montgomery stood clear of the operation but he did criticise its complexity and scale. Unfortunately, he did not apply his own insights in conceptualising Operation MARKET GARDEN where similar planning faults created an even worse Allied defeat.

In short, Operation AGREEMENT failed but the SIG men did not.

As individuals, however, they fought on with passion against German forces. The commander, Captain Buck, was captured during the Tobruk raid and spent the rest of the war as a PoW. Nevertheless, there were early claims that he escaped quickly because he was allegedly involved in the post-raid debrief back in Cairo. Another AGREEMENT survivor, however, Charles Coles, said he met Buck at a PoW camp near Salerno. Coles remembered Buck as a handsome fellow with a neat moustache and a military bearing but he was somewhat 'strange and remote'; all the other PoWs complained endlessly about the lack of food but Buck seemed uninterested and still had the energy to teach fencing lessons. Of course, he was still up to his escape artist act but did not get far from Salerno. Coles later acted as an usher for Buck when he married Celia Wardle, a Wren; tragically, she was soon widowed. The heroic young officer was killed in an air crash, near Chard, Somerset, in a flight to Germany on 22 November 1945. As a German speaker he had been posted to work on occupation duties. The RAF Liberator crashed shortly after take-off from RAF Merryfield near Ilminster.

Buck's Number Two, David Russell, had been the last survivor of the Tobruk raid to reach Allied lines; he was picked up on 18 November 1942 by a squadron of South African armoured cars and taken, in a bad way, to a hospital. He discharged himself from hospital and was soon back on active service. Russell was murdered in Yugoslavia, apparently by ostensible allies, Tito's partisans, in August 1943, while working for the Special Operations Executive. Its 13,000 members were often dubbed 'Churchill's Secret Army' or more caustically the 'Ministry for Ungentlemanly Warfare'. Churchill also sponsored a family of commandos that came originally from No. 2 Commando – the offspring were the SAS, SBS and the Parachute Regiment and, relevant to this story, X Troop, consisting of Jewish volunteers. Some SIG survivors fought on with the commandos in the Balkans, Italy and the Adriatic. J. Kennedy, better known to his mates as 'Chunky' Hillman (aka Steiner), had survived the Tobruk raid and earned both the MC and MM. As we saw, his fluent Arabic helped the small party led by Lieutenant T.B.

Langton to finally yomp to Allied lines. The Senussi Arabs who helped them knew that Italians used to pose as British escapees. Hillman's politeness and his fluent Arabic with a strong Palestinian accent were all unlikely in an Italian spy. Eventually, the Austrian Hillman went on to command a security unit in occupied Germany.

Steiner and Tiefenbrunner and perhaps twelve other SIG men joined the SAS and some served secretly after the war finished – again under the aegis of Churchill, who was by then leader of the opposition, not prime minister.[6] Tiefenbrunner did not take part in the Tobruk raid, but he did become a sergeant in the SAS. During a deep penetration raid in Tunisia, designed to link up with American forces, he was captured and was sent via Italy to Stalag 351 in Hanover, where he pretended to be a French-Canadian born in Montreal. His cover survived until his camp was liberated by the British. He later discovered that both his parents had been killed in the camps.

Some SIG survivors, including Tiefenbrunner, fought in Israel's War of Independence. Buck had previously tried to tempt him to join an SAS operation against the Japanese but it was one fight he chose to decline. Karl Kahane had joined both the SAS and SBS and then fought in the Aegean with the famous Anders Lassen who won a posthumous VC. At Santorini, for example, Kahane was by far the oldest member of the raiding party but played a key role in killing or capturing members of the German garrison there. Later he helped found the Israel Defence Forces' paratrooper brigade.[7]

Again, Orde Wingate's dream had been fulfilled.

Chapter Four

X Troop

Origins of the Commandos

After the Fall of France in 1940, Winston Churchill wanted to set up a 'foreign legion' of 5,000 foreign soldiers serving in the British Army. Lord Mountbatten was said to have further developed the idea into forming a specific German-speaking commando unit. This became known as No. 3 (or X) Troop of 10 (Inter-Allied) Commando.

Mountbatten, later Chief of Combined Operations (1941–43), had a bad habit of stealing other people's ideas but he also had a genuine personal reason for backing a German-speaking unit. He remembered vividly, and bitterly, how his own German connections had impacted on his own family in the Great War. In short, he wanted to prove that there could be some good (and useful) Germans.

Commando raids were one of the few ways the British could strike back on land in occupied Europe in the early stages of the Second World War. Churchill advocated the concept because of his own personal experience in the Second South African War when the successful Boer mounted commandos ran circles around the conventional imperial forces. By 1940 nearly everybody had got in on the act – even the Home Guard (unfairly lampooned in the *Dad's Army* TV series) was used to create special units for guerrilla action in the event of an invasion and occupation. (These units were, however, separate from the Home Guard; they were dubbed Auxiliary Units or GHQ Auxiliary Units.)

Also, many members of the French, Dutch, Belgian, Norwegian, Polish and other exiled armies wanted 'to have a go' at the Germans. They spoke the local languages, had insider knowledge of their countries and definitely had a score to settle. Some were recruited into the Special Operations Executive, whose agents Churchill promised 'would set Europe ablaze'. Churchill also put so clearly the idea of commandos attacking the coastal areas of the continent: 'There comes out of the sea from time to time a hand of steel which plucks the German sentries from their posts with growing efficiency.'

The advantages of native *German-speaking* commandos were obvious. They could act as interpreters on raids, shouting out contradictory orders to confuse defenders and instantly interrogating prisoners of war to secure live battlefield intelligence as well as interpret captured documents. They could also be trained to be experts on German weapons, military structures and deployments. For similar reasons, a Japanese commando unit was debated but that never got off the ground.

Nearly all the Germans who became British commandos were Jews, although there was also a handful of Christian opponents of Nazism involved. This was despite some anti-Semitism in the British high command. And, of course, genuine security concerns were involved in recruiting enemy aliens into elite special forces of the British Army. Under Defence Regulation 18, thousands of refugees, many of them Jewish, were interned. Some were shipped to Canada and Australia under atrocious conditions. Jewish refugees who were sent to Canada and Australia had a tough time, often treated far less well than German PoWs.

Although the German aliens were interned throughout Britain as well as Canada and Australia, one of the most interesting internment centres was the Hutchinson Camp in Douglas, Isle of Man. Most of the prisoners were Jews or opponents of the Nazis. It soon became known as the 'Artists' Camp' because so many artists as well as musicians were inmates. One of the inmates went on to form the Amadeus Quartet but more important for the war effort was the optician Horst Archenhold who designed the periscope that was used to turn the Duplex-Drive Sherman tanks into amphibious craft on D Day. And yet, despite the artistic and sporting flourishes (one of the inmates had been a member of the British Olympic team in 1936), the general atmosphere was one of frustration and despair. A large number of inmates committed suicide in internment in England and Australia and Canada. This was all perfect propaganda for the Germans. As Hitler said in 1940:

> The British have detained in concentration camps, the very people we found it necessary to detain. Where are those much-vaunted democratic liberties of which the English boast?

The Hutchinson Camp was emptied of aliens in March 1944 and it became, somewhat ironically, a German PoW camp.

As the invasion scare began to lift, however, some of the interned aliens in Category C (considered safe from a security point of view) had been allowed to join the Pioneer Corps. The so-called Loyal Alien Companies undertook manual work such as unloading coal for power stations, working on railways or repairing bomb damage. They styled themselves the 'King's Own Loyal Enemy Aliens'. Many of those who joined X Troop were Pioneers who wanted to fight back directly against Hitler.

Life in the Pioneer Corps was not great especially for those who were itching to fight the Nazis. But it was far better than internment in the UK, or the Dominions. The Pioneer Corps consisted of the best and worst of human material. The mentally ill and criminals were mixed with conscientious objectors and 'enemy' aliens. Some of the aliens, such as Arthur Koestler, were, or became, famous intellectuals.

Over 80,000 Jews, including 10,000 *Kindertransport*, were accepted into Britain. The German-speaking commandos, X Troop, with an initial complement of eighty-seven, were nearly all Jewish. That just a small number were selected attested to the very high quality, mentally and physically, of the X Troopers. The overall unit, No. 10 (Inter-Allied Commando), included the following volunteers: French (No. 1); Dutch (No. 2); Belgian (No. 4); Norwegian (No. 5); Polish (No. 6) and Yugoslavian (No. 7) Troops. No. 3 Troop was originally called the British Troop but it was more usually termed X Troop – consisting of German-speaking commandos.

Training

The spiritual home of the Cameron clan, Achnacarry House, in the Scottish Highlands, fifteen miles north of Fort William, was taken over as the Commando HQ in January 1942 'for the duration', although the first intake arrived in March 1942. Irregular warfare had been taught previously when British soldiers were trained both for SOE operations abroad and secret stay-at-home units to resist a German invasion. The commandos, however, were conventional regular soldiers who were taught unconventional skills.

Commandos were expected to show determination and enthusiasm under all conditions; plus, they were expected to develop or possess a keen sense of personal responsibility and self-reliance besides the obvious demands for mental and physical fitness. They had to display an ability to fight in a large formation in conventional war as well perform well in small teams of raiders. They would have to work hard to earn the coveted green beret that was a symbol of elitism and self-discipline as well as military prowess.

Commandos were treated as individuals who were expected to think for themselves. That applied whatever the rank or background. Or class. This was a big change from British military tradition that assumed that only those with a private education were capable of clear decision-making and command and, of course, initiative.

The first to arrive in the Scottish Highlands was a group of French marines. Some of them had volunteered to avoid military prison – most were tough renegades. One was called officially 'Private Boulanger' but he had *Pas de Chance* tattooed on his forehead – he answered to that when he was called on parade.

Battle experience

In early 1943 aliens in the Pioneer Corps were allowed to join other regiments. German-speaking Jews, however, had already been added to raiding parties, including on the ill-fated Dieppe raid in August 1942.

Operation JUBILEE was a cock-up worthy of comparison with the Charge of the Light Brigade, although the fiasco in the Crimean War was on a much smaller scale in terms of casualties. Most of the Dieppe casualties were Canadian; just as at Passchendaele, the Dominion was to pay a high price for British mistakes. Lord Mountbatten always argued that the lessons learned at Dieppe were utterly vital for the preparation of the successful Normandy landings. That is hard to justify except for the one major secret of the raid. It was a heavily disguised and very costly 'Pinch Op' where some of the German-speaking commandos were supposed to seize one of the new four-rotor Enigma code machines and the related codebooks and rotor-setting sheets. Five German-speaking commandos were involved, both to read the relevant documents and, if necessary, find them via interrogation. Historians have debated this for many years but, in 2021, Leah Garrett in her excellent book on X Troop confirmed the Pinch theory by using as evidence one of the five German speakers who survived Dieppe.[1] She cites an after-action report by Maurice Latimer (his cover name). Two German-speaking commandos were captured and one was badly wounded; one got back to Blighty and the fifth was killed. The snatch operation was a failure.

But one important thing was achieved by a Jewish radar expert, Jack Nissenthall, who was guarded by twelve Canadian soldiers. They had been instructed to kill him rather than let him be captured because he knew so much about British radar technology. This order to kill in event of possible capture was probably unique in the war. He was not even given Canadian ID or a back story should he fall into German hands. Jack Nissenthall, from Bow in London, was selected to enter the Pourville radar station to gain vital intelligence on the new German Freya radar. Because of the heavy fighting, Nissenthall and his Canadian bodyguards could not get into the station but the RAF technician, with no combat training, managed, under fire, to crawl around the back of the station, climb the transmitter mast and cut all the telephone wires leading to the station. This forced the Germans to use radio transmission which the British picked up, enabling the Allies to learn a great deal about the location and density of German radar along the channel coast and later to develop jamming technology. Nissenthall managed to get back to Britain with just one surviving bodyguard. Nissenthall, who later changed his name to Nissen, never received any award for his amazing bravery in achieving the single success in a major British Snafu.

Three VCs were earned in the raid and, as a piece of military history trivia, US Army Ranger Corporal Frank Koons became the first American soldier in the Second World War to receive a British award for bravery in action, the Military Medal. The raid also produced the first American fatalities of the war in Europe.

Shortly after the Dieppe fiasco, British commandos raided Sark. The Channel Islands were the only part of the British Isles (though they are Crown Dependencies, not official parts of the UK) occupied by the Germans. So little was known about the fiercely independent island that, when the Germans first landed in 1940, the Wehrmacht officers had to wire their superiors in Berlin to find out if Sark was even technically at war with the Third Reich.

On 3/4 October 1942 a small group of commandos landed at night from MTB 344 (nicknamed 'The Little Pisser') which had the ability to run fast noisily (33 knots) but with quiet auxiliary engines for close-to-shore work. Some of the troops were from No. 12 Commando and a handful from the SOE. Even the definitive book on the raid by Eric Lee, *Operation Basalt*, could not list all the other ranks among the dozen raiders because of the secrecy at the time, especially about German-speaking Jewish commandos. On the balance of probability, at least one or two German-speakers were on the raid. One of the most famous SF soldiers, Anders Lassen, also took part in the raid; he killed a sentry with his treasured commando knife although he was also obsessed with the use of the bow and arrow. (As a Dane, he was one the few non-Commonwealth soldiers to be awarded the VC, posthumously, in the very final days of the war.) Part of the mission was to capture prisoners to be taken back to England for interrogation. Prisoners were indeed taken and bound, but one naked prisoner escaped and raised the alarm (they had been asleep in the middle of the night). One partially-clothed prisoner, however, was taken back on board the MTB to England.

During the Dieppe raid, the Germans had captured the Allied plan – badly hidden on the beach by a surrendering senior officer. According to the German version, the plans instructed that German prisoners should have their hands tied. This was brought to the attention of the Führer, who was incensed by the apparent execution of Germans whose hands had been bound. This led to the shackling of Canadian prisoners from the Dieppe raid, which then prompted the shackling of some German PoWs in Canada. More importantly, the Sark raid was supposed to have led to the infamous *Kommandobefehl* by Hitler to execute all captured Allied commandos – after any necessary interrogation. This inspired a number of German war crimes against captured Allied commandos. Dieppe was a great propaganda victory for Berlin while, by contrast, Sark seemed a tragi-comedy. Although the first deportation had occurred in the previous September, as reprisals for British actions in Iran, many more Channel Islanders were deported soon after, some to work in Germany. The ruler of Sark, Dame Sybil Hathaway, observed acidly that it all 'seemed a heavy price to pay for the capture of one prisoner and a copy of the *Guernsey Evening Press*'. Further deportations linked to the raid were carried out in February 1943.

The Sark raid, Operation BASALT, was clearly more than a footnote in military history and not just because some of the prisoners had been bound on the tiny island. Both Hitler and Churchill took a disproportionate interest in all the Channel Islands. Hitler delighted in the occupation of a part of the British Isles and called it the 'model occupation' – presumably in anticipation of control of all the British Isles. He intended the islands to be one huge holiday camp for German workers after the war. Guernsey and Jersey enjoyed a modicum of reasonable German treatment, unless you were Jewish or Russian, and also a degree of collaboration. But on Alderney large slave-worker camps were established with grossly inhuman treatment, especially for Russian PoWs. Hitler insisted on very expensive and massive fortifications on the islands. It became known as his *Inselwahn* – 'island madness'. The Führer boasted: 'Now we have our foot inside the door of the British Empire.'

The Channel Islands were often described by the occupiers as a 'paradise' not least because they were largely off limits for RAF bombing raids (bombing raids did happen but mostly against shipping and the harbours). The Germans came to dub it as the biggest air raid shelter in Europe. The relative calm was one reason why Churchill was obsessed with Operation BASALT. The day after the raid the prime minister ordered the commando officer in charge to report to him in London for a private meeting.

Besides SOE, the raiders came from No. 62 Commando, also called the Small Scale Raiding Force (SSRF). It was based in Anderson Manor, near Poole in Dorset. The operation did manage to grab one prisoner from the 300 Germans on the island, a success of sorts after the disastrous previous mission when all the raiders were killed or captured. A number of the SSRF were later executed under the terms of the highly illegal Hitler Commando Order. In contrast, the one captured German prisoner from Sark, Herman Weinreich, spent time in the Cage at Latchmere House but he did get back to Germany in one piece in February 1947.

A second raid on Sark ensued on 27/28 December 1943 as part of a series of raids on the French coast and the Channel Islands, Operation HARDTACK. The second Sark intervention resulted in two commandos being killed and one injured in a minefield and the raid was aborted. Of the six commandos, mainly from No. 10 Commando, who climbed the cliffs only one, a sergeant, was unscathed.

The Welsh experience

A handful of Dieppe survivors were asked to join the nucleus of what became officially known as No. 3 (or X) Troop of 10 Commando that comprised, at the start, mainly German-speaking Czechs from the Sudetenland. The first seven or eight commando privates were brought to Wales on 24 July 1942.

The man put in charge of 3 Troop was a Welsh fitness fanatic called Bryan Hilton-Jones. He combined academic and physical prowess as well as being unable to resist a sporting challenge – he started young as a climber in Snowdonia, where his father was a doctor in nearby Caernarfon. Hilton-Jones had taken a first-class degree in the Modern Languages Tripos at Cambridge just before the war; inter alia, he spoke almost flawless German. He was a very quiet man who did not waste words – he led by example. Lieutenant, later Captain, Hilton-Jones regularly displayed his brilliance as a rock climber as many of his troops were to discover, to their despair or sense of terror, around the rocky slopes of Bethesda, North Wales.

Hilton-Jones's best friend after the war, Kevin Fitzgerald, a fellow climber, said of him in an obituary:

> No one could tire him. Many so-called hard men were glad to fall back a little after the first five or six hours. They could outclimb him (some of them) but never outwalk him. He had a map of Wales in his head and never failed to select the hardest, longest distance between any two Welsh points. It was always worth it; he was the perfect companion.

Besides his climbing obsessions, especially in Bethesda, Hilton-Jones used the walls of Harlech Castle as an initiation test for his trainees. They had to scale the castle walls, at night, and the OC did not tell the trigger-happy and over-zealous Home Guard occupants of the castle about any possible nocturnal visitors. Hilton-Jones had a sense of humour but above all he inspired in his men a level of respect that bordered on hero worship. Some of his commandos likened him to Lawrence of Arabia while others feared his physical stoicism. But the vast majority of X Troop remembered him very fondly after the war. He was always called 'The Skipper'.

In a recent interview with the author (11 June 2022), Hilton-Jones's daughter Nerys also clearly hero-worshipped her father, long after his death at 51 in a car crash. 'He was very loving to his family but he was as hard as nails physically.'

Initially The Skipper's Troop was confusingly called the 'English Troop'. The OC was Welsh and Welsh-speaking and there were one or two English officers – the rest were largely German, Austrians and

Czechs with a sprinkling of Poles and Hungarians. Churchill was an enthusiastic supporter and is alleged to have said: 'Because they will be unknown warriors – they must perforce be considered an unknown quantity. Since the algebraic symbol for the unknown is X, let us call them X troops.'

Most of the new Jewish recruits were billeted in private homes around Aberdyfi (in English, Aberdovey). In early 1943 the first wave of forty-three men arrived; the second wave consisted of sixteen soldiers and the final wave comprised thirteen aspiring commandos. Over 350 men were short-listed but the MI5 clearances were thorough and very time-consuming. In the end only eighty-seven men were recruited in the first intakes.

It was decided not to put the aspiring commandos into a central barracks, so the local police visited homes in and around Aberdyfi, which was almost entirely Welsh-speaking. One policeman used polite and formal chapel Welsh but he had met with a stern rebuff from a certain lady, inevitably named Mrs Jones.

'Why can't they go back to their own homes, Constable?' she said in the Celtic tongue.

'They can't go back as Jerry has taken everything.'

The light finally dawned on Mrs Jones – she had assumed they were *real* foreigners, English soldiers. So, she said: *'Roeddwn i'n meddwl eich bod chi'n siarad am filwyr* Saesneg. *Baswn i'n falch o helpu.'*

Mrs Jones was more than happy to help *non-English* foreigners.

Anti-Semitism was not a factor despite the anti-English Welsh nationalism and pacifist religious traditions. The oldest inhabitant of Aberdyfi in 2022, Myra Hayler, at '99 and three-quarters', as she put, said that it didn't matter if they were Jewish – 'They were our boys.'[2]

The troopers were anyway told to be careful to hide their pasts. (The Skipper had instructed his men never to keep diaries but some did and produced exhilarating memoirs.) Maybe the habitually curious Welsh hosts did peak at diaries and correspondence but usually kept schtum. Sometimes the landladies cottoned on, especially as one was Jewish herself. At the regular dances, the sober, educated and usually charming

X Troopers were a big hit with the local females. And, in at least two cases, the Jewish soldiers married their landladies' daughters: Max Laddy (Lewinski) and Dicky Tenant (Richard Trojan). Laddy's pregnant wife, Dorothy, was widowed shortly after D Day. Dorothy gave birth to her daughter Christine at roughly the same time that her husband was killed in France. Dorothy never married again and her daughter visits Aberdyfi every Remembrance Sunday.

X Troop trained together but they did not fight as a single unit, despite – or because of – being some of the best-trained special forces in the British Army. They were also some of the best educated academically. Besides their rock-climbing skills and expertise in German weaponry, they developed more esoteric skills such as driving trains and picking locks. Their most important skill, however, was still their command of German. A handful of X Troop had served in the German or Austrian armies. Before the anti-Jewish laws, it had been common for Jews to spend a 'gap year' in the armed forces between school and university.

X Troop came under the overall command of 10 (Inter-Allied) Commando based in Harlech. The commandos sometimes trained and paraded together. Each unit had its own customised version of British uniforms and even held their rifles at different angles. Drill was different and so were the parade-ground languages. Confusion ranged across the rank badges. For example, the highest-ranking NCO in the French component was their sergeant-major whose gold braid was so lavish that he could have been, and probably was, mistaken for a rear admiral. Inevitably, the French were the most individualistic and bloody-minded and they didn't like taking orders from non-French officers.

Initially, 10 Commando was considered a bit of a ghetto, not an elite unit. That caricature changed, however. The performance of the early raiders, even when the mission failed, such as at Dieppe, soon made all the difference.

All the commandos had to be tough but the Jewish soldiers had to be extra determined, not least because of their double jeopardy. The *Kommandobefehl* of 18 October 1942 stated that any commandos captured on raids would not be treated as ordinary PoWs. They were to be handed over to the Gestapo for possible torture and certain execution. As discussed earlier, the SIG Jewish fighters would be killed immediately if discovered in German uniform, except for a possible brief reprieve for interrogation under torture.

The first X Trooper to be recruited was George Lane (Lanyi), who had already served in SOE. The first sergeant in the unit had film-star good looks and build. Originally from Hungary, he was brought up a Catholic by his wealthy Christian father and by his Jewish mother. An Olympic-level sportsman, he was fluent in Hungarian, German and French and was well-read. After arriving in the UK in 1935, he had studied at Oxford and the University of London, plus he moved in high circles, where he was asked if he could play cricket. Joking that he was the best cricketer in Hungary, he was accepted into the Grenadier Guards. Despite his contacts and later marriage to one of the wealthiest Jews in England, Miriam Rothschild, even the dashing George Lane still had to suffer a year in the Pioneer Corps before being recruited into the SOE. In his memoirs, Lane noted that he had been trusted only with a broomstick and shovel in the Pioneer Corps and then he suddenly became a well-armed spy for the British. He said what most of the X Troopers must have thought, 'Who said the English are logical?'

When they started sorting out suitable men, Lane said that, besides brains and fitness, 'they were looking for people whose local knowledge and languages and hatred for Hitler were very much in evidence.'

One of the later X Troopers was Peter Arany who was brought up in Vienna and then fled to England after the *Anschluss*. He adopted the *nom de guerre* of Peter Masters. In his revealing memoir, *Striking Back*, Masters/Arany explained why he was so keen to become a commando:

Shocked by history, desperate and in danger, we were threatened first by Hitler – that vast unswerving scourge, that creator of hell on earth. Then, by our own choice, we fought for the opportunity to counter seemingly unsurmountable odds. Those who died preferred their fate to being gassed and cremated by the Nazi brute. Those of us who survived feel that the remainder of our lives is a bonus to be cherished.

The theme of the memoir was the determination to fight back at all costs. Masters said simply: 'In the antithesis of the "lambs to the slaughter" we fought and many of us died.'[3]

That burning desire for retribution was one reason why so many Jewish commandos dreaded the one phrase during their training: RTU (Returned to Unit), which meant that they could not be elite fighters against Hitler's forces. And the training was very tough – including the use of live ammunition. They were all given new English names and elaborate back stories that involved English birth while the religion on their identity discs was Church of England. Sometimes, if they were captured their aliases held, and in one or two cases their weird English accents were passed off as Welsh accents to German interrogators with less-than-perfect English. In this case, the soldiers' courtship of local girls provided an inadvertent military bonus.

Masters recounted in his memoir a story of a night-time reconnaissance exercise. The small town of Tywyn was six miles from their training centre at Aberdyfi. The Royal Air Force had an airfield and a small base there. Masters and his team were ordered to infiltrate the base unseen and unheard and return with details of what had been observed. The RAF were not told of the exercise, so the troopers could be expected to be fired on, if seen – 'Well, there is a war on, you know.' Just to complicate matters, the RAF base was protected by a minefield.

The trainees had to be on parade as usual at 08.00, all spick and span. The night infiltration had been successful and one of the commandos, *nom de guerre* Tommy Farr, stood to attention wearing a Women's Auxiliary Air Force blue hat on his fair hair.

Masters commented that Farr had not been satisfied with just accomplishing his prescribed task of getting into the well-guarded compound and then sneaking into the WAAF huts to count the occupants. Farr was determined to show off his captured trophy. Masters continued:

The Skipper took one look at him. 'Farr, you will proceed unseen to Tywyn RAF base forthwith and replace stolen RAF property precisely where you found it. Then report back to me in exactly two hours. On the double. Dismissed.

Some of X Troop were deployed on secret recce missions before D Day in June 1944 prior to the biggest land, sea and air operation in military history.

George Lane commanded three operations in a series of raids dubbed Operation TARBRUSH in May 1944. Part of the missions was to check on supposedly new mines laid along French beaches. Lane reported on the Teller mines but his information was not believed, so he went back to the same beach the next night and then the next, but on the third time with a sapper officer, Roy Wooldridge. The now Lieutenant George Lane was captured with Wooldridge near the French port of Cayeux. The Germans were very interested in the capture of a commando and so Lane endured lengthy interrogation, but no rough handling, by the German army, not Gestapo. Lane later said: 'I figured they might just possibly detect a Hungarian speaking English but never a Hungarian superimposing a Welsh accent on top of that.'

It worked.

After the initial Wehrmacht interrogation, a German officer came into Lane's cell and told him he was going to meet a very important person. The German asked whether Lane would behave like 'an officer and a gentleman'.

Lane relied simply, 'I always do.'

That VIP was Field Marshal Erwin Rommel. The German commander wanted to see for himself what a commando looked like. Rommel made a few asides about 'gangster commandos' and then tea was served.

'And how is my old friend, Montgomery?'

'Very well, sir, as far as I know.'

'You really think there is going to be an invasion?'

'So I read in *The Times*, sir.'

After a pleasant chat, Rommel promised that Lane and his companion would be taken safely to a PoW camp. Despite various initial attempts by the Gestapo, Rommel's promise of safe conduct and treatment ensured that both X Troopers survived as PoWs until the end of the war. When he arrived at the first PoW camp, however, his heavy accent and his reluctance to reveal his unusual adventures in SOE and X Troop, and having no standard regimental background, initially made his fellow officers very suspicious until Lane confided in the senior British officer in the camp.

D Day and after

One officer and forty-three other ranks from X Troop were deployed on the D Day landings. Of this original group, twenty-seven were killed, wounded or taken prisoner. They did not fight as a unit but were split up to act as forward recce and also as frontline interrogators.

Peter Masters landed at Queen section of Sword Beach on the first day. This was now his chance to strike back. He said to himself that he felt 'well trained and definitely a better-than-even match for what I was likely to encounter'. Carrying a tommy gun in one hand and a bike in the other, he waded knee-deep ashore. He was also carrying his rations, a blanket and a full-size pick-axe. Others had spades but the commandos had reckoned that the army-issue entrenching tool was not good enough to dig a hole quickly enough.

In his memoir Masters had enough time to observe the famous eccentricity of the officer class. He noted:

> Our brigadier, Lord Lovat, was walking about the assembly area, urging people on. [He was David Stirling's cousin and was every bit as mad if not madder.] Lovat seemed perfectly at ease, in spite of the shooting and other noise. He carried no weapon other than his Colt .45 pistol, which was still in his holster. Instead, he had a walking stick, a long slim piece of forked wood. Later a Scottish Highlander explained to me that it was a wading stick, used for helping to keep one's balance when fly fishing for trout or salmon.

Most of the commandos had not seen action before and the experience of death everywhere was very new, especially when comrades were dying around them. 'We were shocked to see dead parachutists hanging in the trees. Even the sight of dead cattle in the fields adjacent to our route, belly up and bloated in rigor mortis, was upsetting.'

Masters and other X Troopers remembered The Skipper's advice, 'Make a nuisance of yourself.' It took a little while but soon the value of their recce and language skills as well as knowledge of German army routines were understood by the various commanders to whom they were attached.

Often, they were sent on almost suicidal missions. Masters had been ordered to walk alone into a village where a unit of Germans were taking cover behind a low wall. He remembered an American film, *Gunga Din*, he had seen starring Cary Grant. When surrounded by rebel Afghan tribesmen in the Khyber Pass, the Hollywood hero shouts to them, 'You are all under arrest.'

There wasn't cover for Masters so he decided to brazen it out. *'Ergebt Euch alle! Alle 'raus!'* He shouted at the top of his voice, trying to sound German, not Austrian. *'Ihr seid vollkommen umzingelt – Ihr habt keine Chance. Werft Eure Waffen fort und kommt mit den Händen hoch 'raus wenn Ihr weiter leben wollt. Der Krieg ist aus für Euch.'* The war was over, he told them, they were surrounded and should throw down their weapons.

The outrageous bluff didn't work for long but the amazing lull allowed time for Masters's comrades to arrive in sufficient numbers for him to survive the ensuing firefight.

As the X Troop commandos crawled and marched through Normandy, they were sometimes serving alongside other commandos, notably the French who fought as a unit. The Jewish troopers knew what they were fighting *against* but they were not always sure what they were fighting *for*. As Masters put it, 'We wanted to fight our oppressors and had few illusions about returning to our countries but our French commando comrades were liberating their homeland.'

X Troop members had much more freedom of movement and individual initiative than other Allied troops and so moved around more and volunteered more. As a result, their casualties were very high. During the first few weeks the rain and mosquitoes were more troublesome than the German defenders but soon the Wehrmacht fought back stubbornly once they had got over the initial shock of an invasion in Normandy rather than around Calais.

After a few months of hard fighting, X Troop survivors were brought home for R and R. But they were soon re-deployed in the fighting through Italy from Sicily. They were used extensively in the Low Countries and the fighting across the Rhine into the heart of Germany. According to Antony Beevor's authoritative account, twenty Jewish German commandos joined the initial parachute Pathfinders at Arnhem on 17 September 1944. Garrett's excellent, if understandably somewhat partisan, account emphasises that the X Troopers very rarely lost their tempers, especially with prisoners. They were not, she says, mindlessly aggressive as in Quentin Tarantino's film, *Inglourious Basterds*. Beevor, however, quotes a number of examples of bloodlust, not least the killing of surrendering German prisoners.[4]

As the X Troopers moved across their former homelands and countered the death camps, the truth about Nazism was far, far worse than they had ever imagined. As Garrett puts it: 'The so-called civilised Germans and Austrians they had gone to school with had, in a few short years, become the least civilised people to ever walk the earth.'

The Troop was officially disbanded in September 1945 but some went on to join the SAS (when it was *officially* disbanded) and also the Royal Marine Commandos. Many joined specialised intelligence units tracking down senior Nazis. Fred Jackson, a fairly new recruit to X Troop interrogated Rudolf Hoess, the commander of Auschwitz. After the harrowing job he was given a week's leave. Jackson confessed that he got drunk every day of his leave. 'He was the man who killed my mother.'

They were a somewhat secretive group, not least because captured commandos were usually killed and the Gestapo would try to wipe out any of their surviving families in the Reich. And because they fought alongside other, varying, units as individuals they were often not in a position to be put forward for honours by any commanding officers. Nevertheless, of the 130 men who passed through X Troop, nineteen became officers, often commissioned for bravery in the field. (This was despite Montgomery's drive to prevent battlefield commissions, as he wanted a fully professional officer corps.) X Troop earned, inter alia, one MC, one MM, one Croix de Guerre and one BEM.

Of the forty-four men from X Troop who saw action in Normandy, twenty-one were killed in action and many of their replacements were seriously wounded. The Skipper was seriously wounded in the stomach when he parachuted into Normandy but he was treated well in a German hospital in France and eventually recovered in hospital in England (typically Hilton-Jones went out of his way to help the German army doctor who had befriended him and later was made a British PoW). In September 1944 The Skipper was recovering in the Millar Ward of the Royal Hospital, Wolverhampton, and was hoping to be discharged after a long recovery from serious stomach wounds. He wrote to a fellow officer who had been in X Troop:

It is probable the King will not require my paralytic services any more … and so I may, after some leave, etc. join the unemployed like yourself. But I can't for the life of me think of any exam I could possibly pass after five years in the army, except perhaps on the theory of pure and applied bullshit … . Despite the great attachment to the idea of leave I shall probably try to get down to Eastbourne [where the HQ of X Troop was then based] fairly soon if only to try to justify my majority which is almost as phoney as my MC.[5]

Many of the X Troopers then served in the British occupation zones. Initially some were involved in the hunt for Heinrich Himmler, while others tried to track down advanced scientists to help with the future struggle with Russia. Some disguised themselves as German Nazi resistance, especially the so-called Werewolves.

Lieutenant Manfred Gans managed to fulfil the ambition of most X Troopers who dreamed of saving at least some of their families from the Nazi abominations. With one driver in a jeep, Gans managed to cross various occupation zones and German army-held areas to reach Theresienstadt camp in Czechoslovakia where he located, and organised the rescue of, his parents. En route, he also managed to enlist the help not only of generous Americans but also Yiddish-speaking Red Army officers.

Ronnie Gilbert (Hans-Julius Guttman) was an X Trooper who was appointed MBE for his years of service in the new Federal German intelligence machine. Even the Germans wanted to give him a medal for tracking down war criminals. It was a fitting legacy for a young man who had been forced to help demolish the synagogue of his hometown of Singen during *Kristallnacht.*

Despite their amazing military service, the British government was churlish in helping to allow the X Troop survivors to become naturalised citizens. Despite The Skipper's strenuous efforts and some top brass intervention, it was not until September 1946 that the German troopers were naturalised. Some, like Masters, moved to the US; he talked and wrote about his experiences and brought up his children as fully Jewish. Many former X Troopers remained in Britain. Perhaps because of the fear of recurrent violent anti-Semitism, even in Britain, some kept their adopted names – and even cover Church of England religion – perhaps out of loyalty to the country which had made them warriors.

In 1999 a memorial was erected to the dead of X Troop in Penhelig Park in Aberdyfi. Some of the survivors who attended accepted the fact that crosses instead of the *Magen David* should mark the names. (There are no names on the memorial.) Others objected, remembering the anger some had felt when their comrades had fallen in the first days of the Normandy invasion. Three X Troopers had been buried temporarily with crosses in a churchyard. In the end, despite the protests of Martin Sugarman, of the Jewish Museum in London, the local council did not add the *Magen David* to the memorial. It was perhaps an ironic comment on the final integration of the men who had been forced to flee Germany and had sometimes been forced into awful camps in the UK and worse ones in Australia and Canada, and then made aliens, forbidden to bear arms, and yet finally had become the finest of British special forces.[6]

Chapter Five

The Ritchie Boys

The Americans were slow to adopt the British military intelligence approach to deploying German-speaking Jews. Yet long before Pearl Harbor, General George C. Marshall, who became the US Army Chief of Staff the day Germany invaded Poland, had become seriously concerned about the poor condition of the army's intelligence training. Never a combat veteran, he was, however, a genius at training and organising; Winston Churchill later called him the 'organiser of victory' in the Second World War. In the spring of 1941, he sent a group of officers to Britain to study military intelligence training there. As a result of their report, a centralised location for the training of interrogators, interpreters and translators was set up: Camp Ritchie, in remote Maryland but not too far from Washington DC. It was shrouded in secrecy almost as intense as the Manhattan Project, the development of the atom bomb, that was commenced in Oak Ridge, Tennessee, in the summer of 1941.

General Marshall was something of an admirer of some of the British Army's methods; he did not, however, develop the specific training of German-speaking Jews in a special forces' role, either as commandos or as a pseudo unit such as the Special Interrogation Group in North Africa. The US had little input into the early days of the British intelligence war because much mutual suspicion festered among the allies, as was dramatised just after the war ended when British involvement in the joint atom bomb project was cold-bloodedly axed. This was a shattering blow to the British confidence in US-UK intelligence sharing.

* * *

In 1926 the Maryland National Guard had selected a site for its summer camps. The Guard purchased 638 acres, with two lakes, and named it after the state governor, Albert C. Ritchie. On 19 June 1942 the US Army took over the camp as its Military Intelligence Training Center. Altogether, nearly 20,000 troops were trained there – many of them became known as the 'Ritchie Boys'.

The War Powers Act of 1922 had previously stopped immigrants joining the armed forces. That law was revised in March 1942: aliens could now fight and die for the American republic. The revised law stated that any immigrants, including enemy aliens, who had served honourably in the armed forces for at least three months were eligible for naturalisation. Previously, all immigrants, even those serving in the military, had been required to be residents of the USA for a minimum of five years. Now those who were enlisted for training in Camp Ritchie were quickly made naturalised citizens. Students were taken to nearby Hagerstown for their oath of loyalty in front of a judge, as part of their naturalisation process.

Of the 20,000 personnel trained in Camp Ritchie, 18 per cent were Jewish; many were US-born and 15 per cent were from Germany and four per cent from Austria. Exactly 1,985 German-born Jews and 493 Austrians attended the camp. The question was not nationality but language skills. Italian speakers and those of Japanese heritage were also part of the Babel's Tower of languages, cultures and traditions in the camp.

The variety of the languages was the first thing that newcomers noticed. The second was the lack of bull. This suited many of the new students, especially the more academically inclined. Many of the Jewish 'campers' were destined to become famous: one of the best known was perhaps J.D. Salinger. His proficiency in French and German meant that he was very useful on his course – usually of eight intensive weeks of training – to become an interrogator of German prisoners of war. Others specialised in the 'OB' course – studying the Order of Battle that required a detailed knowledge of the German army; it was assumed that they would not come across many naval and air force personnel. Many became interrogators and interpreters while others specialised in areas

The Ritchie Boys   69

where languages were not so essential, such as bomb damage assessment and other photographic interpretation skills.

Some of the Jewish Ritchie Boys had begged to join the army, anything to fight back against the Nazis who had driven them out of their homes. But the restrictions on aliens, asylum seekers and other recent immigrants had previously reinforced some xenophobic, and indeed anti-Semitic, elements in the military leadership, especially in military intelligence. But as the graduates of Camp Ritchie took to the field, initially in North Africa, General George Patton summed up the prevailing attitude about the former foreigners: 'They were not only welcome but they were in demand.'

Günther (Guy) Stern had spent an idyllic childhood in Hildesheim, one of the oldest and prettiest towns in northern Germany. Forced to flee to America by the Nazi abominations, he was surprised on his arrival at Camp Ritchie to be greeted at the gate by military policemen speaking flawless German. Other arrivals were astounded to see columns of men in Wehrmacht uniforms with a German sergeant counting *'Links, zwei, drei, vier … '*

As Guy Stern said at the time:

We were fighting an American war, and we were also fighting an intensely personal war. We were in it with every fibre of our being. We worked harder than anyone could have driven us. We were crusaders. This was our war.[1]

Camp Ritchie courses

Thirty-three students graduated from the first eight-week course in October 1942. They were native German-speakers on the IPW-German course for interrogators of prisoners of war. The classes soon grew in size – the thirty-four classes that followed graduated, on average, fifty students a month. Some of the first Ritchie graduates were rushed abroad to take part in Operation TORCH, the Allied invasion of Vichy-controlled French North-West Africa. Other especially talented students did extra courses elsewhere or helped out as instructors in Camp Ritchie.

Although the students were highly driven and worked long hours, it was not all work. Besides being highly motivated, many of the often well-educated students were creative and artistic. For example, Harry Kahn would dress up as a mock Hitler, with a false toothbrush moustache, when they were replicating Nazi rallies for the propaganda section. (After the war, Harry became a professional mime artist.) The off-duty discussions were more like a university than an army camp – where the students might discuss not just German politics but world history, philosophy, music and the arts.

Nevertheless, the days in the classroom or on arduous exercises in the woods were exhausting. Initially, the local farmers were shocked at seeing 'invading' Germans in uniform in Wehrmacht half-tracks but they soon got used to both the 'Germans' and Ritchie Boys in US uniforms getting lost in their area. The Order of Battle course was usually considered the toughest. They learned not just about German weapons and technology but also medals and uniforms. Someone in German regalia would dash into a classroom for a few seconds and then the students would be expected to identify the branch, rank, medals, piping on the cap etc.

On the specialist PoW interrogation course, the students learned to interpret the soldier's pay-book (*Soldat Buch*) that would contain details of campaigns, any wounds and recent leave. The Ritchie Boys' detailed knowledge would be useful to impress a PoW, for example, by casually dropping in the name of the commanding officer. It could have a profound psychological effect. If the prisoner thought the interrogator knew this or that level of detail, then the odd additional fact, perhaps in exchange for a cigarette or a chocolate bar, could be of immediate tactical value and thus save American lives.

The German-speaking students, besides being armed with up-to-date information on the German army, would also have intuitive insights into the prisoners' culture and psyche.

The students on the PoW courses relied on four key points:

They had comprehensive knowledge of the details of the parent unit.
Often prisoners would be interrogated on the frontline. The first

few hours and days were vital as the captured soldiers were often nervous and disorientated.

Bribery was useful. The Ritchie Boys were trained to enter the interrogation room eating a Hershey bar or smoking a cigarette. If the prisoner asked for something to eat or a smoke, the answer would be yes, if the prisoners were co-operative.

The interrogators were also taught to find common interests, for example sport. Sometimes chatting about such pastimes would encourage prisoners to forget the different uniforms.

Fear was also used, when necessary. Yet violence was utterly condemned in the training courses, not just for moral reasons but because torture rarely worked. Most people would say anything to stop the pain. Not all Germans are Nazis, the students were told. But when the students engaged in real interrogations they would nearly always tell frightened PoWs who asked whether they would be tortured, '*We* are not Nazis.'

They were instructed never to touch a prisoner, although they could be shouted at. In the front line, PoWs were sometimes knocked about a bit or threatened with a gun, even if it was merely brandished not used.

The most effective method for dealing with a truly recalcitrant PoW was the threat to hand over the prisoner to the Russians. Germans knew what abominations the Nazis had committed on the eastern front where Russian military prisoners and ordinary citizens alike were treated like cattle, if they were lucky. The German PoWs would do anything to remain captives of the well-provisioned and usually lenient Americans.

Some real prisoners were imported from those captured in North Africa and brought to Camp Ritchie, to give the students some real face time with real German veterans.

Some of the best students were rapidly promoted even during training at Camp Ritchie or other courses. Their rapid promotions to master sergeant used to upset less qualified veterans with longer service. It was always said that the '*needs* of the service' mattered more than the years of service. One Ritchie Boy, after just five months in military intelligence, went from no stripes to six chevrons on his sleeve. And in combat they proved to be distinguished soldiers, often gaining rapid battlefield commissions. They also had the freedom to move around; being in military intelligence, they were rarely challenged, although they were usually attached to divisions and regiments.

Ritchie Boys in action

'To a man, these Jewish exiles were willing to leave their American asylum and return to Europe to fight the Nazis,' was how Bruce Henderson, the author of the definitive book, *The Ritchie Boys*, puts it.[2]

Some were thrown immediately into the campaign against the retreating Germans in North Africa. Others had a cushier posting by joining British military intelligence units in England. Most of the Ritchie Boys were billeted with local families where they were more than happy to share their chocolates and good-quality cigarettes in a country that had endured long and severe rationing.

*   *   *

It is sometimes forgotten how important food is to soldiers. In combat, footwear and food become dominant topics of conversation in nearly all fighting armies. Most American observant Jews found non-kosher food, mixing meat and dairy products, for example, revolting. And even secular Jews found swallowing bacon difficult. Both in the US and UK, when many new Jewish troops faced their first army breakfast, few had not fully realised how Jewish identity was fixed in the mundane realm of food.

Even before facing the impossibility of finding kosher food in the Allied forces, many of the first Jewish immigrants, especially, found the conditions harsh. The *Kindertransport* had arrived in one of the worst winters for years. Many of the German children had become used to central heating at home and usually indoor toilets; it was not so even in middle-class Britain. The diaries of the new arrivals are full of complaints about the constant rain but also of poor treatment and being made to work as domestic skivvies. Most comments recorded were about the inedibility of the food (except for Cadbury's chocolate, which they preferred to the German brands). But they hated what passed for bread.

* * *

Some of the British equivalents of the Ritchie Boys had already been doing reconnaissance of the French coast before D Day. And British Jewish commandos were in the first waves of the amphibious landings. Most Americans had not shared the British commando experience of coastal raids and were often quite green. Werner Angress, for example, was a Ritchie Boy who was getting ready to jump with the 82nd Airborne Division. Werner was sweating under the load – each man had between 50 and 70 pounds of equipment. He had two parachutes, one on his back and a second on his chest. A gas mask was tied to one leg, while a small hoe was tied to the other, although it was always considered too small for digging effective foxholes. Clipped to his chest harness above the reserve chute were two 'frag' (fragmentation) grenades. On his webbing he had a canteen of water, a bayonet, a small medical kit, extra ammunition and a commando knife. Strapped under his front chute was a so-called musette bag that contained water purification tabs, chocolate bars, a shaving kit and extra underwear and socks. It also contained a phosphorus grenade which some of the Ritchie Boys considered inhumane because of the awful burns-induced death they could cause. By contrast, Werner's bag also included his volume of Rudyard Kipling.

Werner was one of the Ritchie Boys who was captured briefly by the Germans, but soon released after the rapid US advance in France. Others were not so lucky. Their training had drilled into them not to talk about their Jewish background in Germany if they were later captured in a German counter-offensive. And some of their surviving family members in Germany and the occupied territories could be severely victimised – even further.

During the December 1944 Ardennes counter-offensive, the Battle of the Bulge or the Rundstedt Offensive, as the Germans called it, two Ritchie interrogators were captured and then identified as probable Jewish interrogators in US service by recently liberated German prisoners. It was at the Bleialf customs house near the German border. Hauptmann Curt Bruns, a fervent Nazi, had commanded his 2nd Battalion of the 293rd Regiment in the 18th Volksgrenadiers for over a year.[3] The two freshly captured American soldiers were Kurt Jacobs and Murray Zappler. When the German officer asked Jacobs why he spoke flawless German, he explained he had been a law student in Berlin. He then tried to use his legal expertise and knowledge of the Geneva Convention to dissuade the Germans from executing them then and there. An infuriated Hauptmann Bruns said, *'Juden haben kein Recht in Deutschland zu leben.'* Bruns ordered his sergeant to line up an impromptu firing squad that shot the two helpless Americans in the back. Hauptmann Bruns, however, was later afforded a proper American military trial and was also executed but by a formal firing squad on 24 June 1945.

Sometimes it was almost impossible for some interrogators not to hint at their background. One interrogator came across a prisoner whom he knew from school in Hildesheim. Because the American soldier was sitting in a darkened section of the room, the German PoW did not recognise him. The former Jewish refugee was desperate to ask if the prisoner knew anything about the family he had left behind. This former schoolmate might have known. But the prisoner was almost immediately sent back to the cage and was not interrogated again by the same American investigator from Hildesheim.

One tough SS prisoner gave in when the American interrogator broke the rules and said that he had been in Dachau and knew how the SS treated prisoners. It was recorded that the PoW 'shat himself, literally'.

Sometimes humour intruded. One Ritchie Boy with para wings on his uniform was told by a captured German paratrooper: 'Paratroopers on both sides should persuade the International Olympic Committee to include parachute jumping in the next Olympic games.' There were, however, more US casualties in glider landings in Normandy than in parachute jumps.

One of the most amusing of the Ritchie Boys' antics was inventing a 'mad Russian liaison officer'. A handful of Soviet officers were indeed attached to Allied HQ but they did not get involved with interrogations, although captured Germans were unlikely to know that. The average German soldier was indoctrinated into believing in the slogan '*Sieg oder Siberien*' – victory or Siberia.

Guy Stern and Fred Howard developed a crazy Russian character who had appeared in the very popular Eddie Cantor radio show and also on the Jack Benny Show. Bert Gordon, originally Barney Gorodetsky a New York Jew, just like Cantor, many of whom had Russian heritage, became known as the 'mad Russian' throughout his theatrical career. The Ritchie Boys adapted all the mannerisms but called their creation Commissar Krukov. They obtained Russian uniforms and medals from Russians freed from German captivity and confiscated German loot. In a tent, which was supposed to be a special liaison office, the final touch was a photograph of Stalin, signed, in Russian, 'To my good friend, Comrade Krukov'.

Guy Stern played the commissar although he did not know a word of Russian but he was a fan of the Eddie Cantor show. If a prisoner proved too truculent, then Fred Howard, with their practised dialogue, would say to the prisoner, 'Reluctantly I now have to take you to Commissar Krukov's tent.'

Krukov (in German): 'You imbecile, what kind of sorry specimen are you bringing me? That Nazi won't even survive the transport to our Siberian salt mines.'

US soldier (in German): 'I must ask you to calm down and respect my uniform and not shout at me or I will take my prisoner back to my office.'

Krukov: 'You will not do that. This room is Russian soil.'[4]

Most prisoners broke on the first visit and definitely on the second when the commissar would get into top foam-flecked gear.

Black humour was often the only way to handle the endless hours of work, physical dangers and, later, the trauma of witnessing the concentration camps. Sometimes the Ritchie Boys would be involved in actual fighting and they would search through the uniforms of dead Germans for documents as well as interview live PoWs. Despite the dangers, not least of constant artillery, the Ritchie Boys were imbued with the typical fatalism, like most front-line soldiers. It was not your time unless the bullet had your name on it, whatever you did. The Ritchie Boys did not generally fear a quick battlefield death. Their desire for some sort of 'payback' meant that many were daily breaking the old soldier's dictum, 'Never Volunteer'. They *did* volunteer for many dangerous roles. What worried the Germans in US uniforms was their Jewish heritage being discovered after being captured and then falling into the hands of, and being tortured by, the Gestapo. As it happened, the well-known case of the two interrogators captured in the Ardennes counter-offensive meant that they were summarily executed by a *Wehrmacht* fanatic. But, unlike falling into the hands of the Gestapo or *Sicherheitsdienst*, that illegal execution was at least swift.[5]

That, of course, would be of little comfort to their families, if they could have known. Typically, many of the German-Jewish refugees sent to safety were the oldest sons, so that, anticipating the worst, the family lineage could be preserved. Most of the Ritchie Boys survived; most of their families in occupied Europe did not.

Fatalism grew among PoWs as well. In the summer of 1944, at the same time as the July plot against Hitler, one of the Ritchie Boys told a front-line American journalist that 90 per cent of PoWs interrogated thought the war was hopeless but only 75 per cent would ever admit it. But the attitude began to change a little as the Allies pushed into Germany – many more Wehrmacht soldiers were more motivated to defend the homeland against the invaders. American intelligence was keen to find out whether the Wehrmacht was preparing to use gas in defence of the homeland. Detailed interrogations by military intelligence discovered that the Germans had considered preparation to defend *against* chemical warfare but they were not preparing to *initiate* it at all themselves.

Orde Wingate – the founder of the Special Night Squads. (*Wikipedia*)

The apotheosis of Wingate's vision: Moshe Dayan, Chief of the Israeli General Staff. (*IDF*)

Special Night Squads: British soldiers in 1938/9.

Captain Herbert Buck, the founder of the Special Interrogation Group. (*Special Forces Roll of Honour*)

Maurice Tiefenbrunner, a key soldier in the SIG, who later joined the SAS. (*Special Forces Roll of Honour*)

SIG soldiers in a German half-track. (*MilitaryImages.Net*)

rom left to right: Dov Cohen, Philip Kogel, Dolph Zeintner, still in their Middle East 51 Commando niform before joining SIG.

British Army in Egypt in 1940.

Long Range Desert Group. (*National Army Museum*)

The LRDG using the favourite 30-cwt Chevrolet. (*National Army Museum*)

Chevrolet: never standardised as each one was customised as the commander saw fit. Firepower was provided by various combinations of Browning, Lewis and Vickers machine guns.

General Erwin Rommel in his Horch staff car. (*German government archives*)

Operation AGREEMENT. Commando Force B at Gilf Kebir outcrop.

Rommel talks to his men in a captured American half-track. (*German government archives*)

HMS *Sikh* was a Tribal-class destroyer that entered service in 1938. She participated in the sinking of the *Bismarck* but was sunk during Operation AGREEMENT. (*Wikipedia*)

The *Afrikakorps* logo.

The disastrous Dieppe Raid, August 1942.

Bryan Hilton-Jones as a captain; he was the CO of X Troop. (*From the Hilton-Jones family collection*)

Hilton-Jones terrified his men in their rock-climbing exercises. (*From the Hilton-Jones family collection*)

George Lane, the Hungarian playboy who became the first sergeant in X Troop. (*Commando Veterans*)

Hilton-Jones ordered a detachment of his X Troop to climb Harlech Castle at night, without informing the trigger-happy Home Guard who were based there. (*Author's picture*)

This British Army Commando Troop initially consisted of eighty-six German-speaking refugees from Nazi oppression who were given fictitious names and identities as British nationals for their own protection and effectiveness. Commanded by Major Hilton-Jones MC, their special duties were reconnaissance, interrogation and intelligence. Deployed singly or in small groups, they rendered distinguished service in the defeat of Hitler's Germany.

Memorial plaque in Penhelig Park, Aberdyfi. (*Author's picture*)

The X Troop memorial in Aberdyfi. (*Author's picture*)

IN
FOR THE
MEMBERS OF
3 TROOP 10 IA
COMMANDO
WHO WERE
WARMLY WELCOMED
IN ABERDYFI
WHILE TRAINING
FOR SPECIAL DUTIES
IN BATTLE
1942-1943
TWENTY WERE
KILLED IN ACTION

Brigadier Ernest Benjamin, the commander of the Jewish Brigade, inspecting his men.

Israel Carmi served in the SIG, Jewish Brigade and IDF. (*Palmach Archives*)

Jewish Brigade troops on top of a Churchill tank in March 1945, near Alfonsine (between the Senio river and the Adriatic).

Jewish Brigade in northern Italy with captured Germans. The Brigade fought in the battles around the Senio river in April 1945. (*Yad Vashem archives*)

US forces landing at Omaha Beach. (*US Army*)

Wehrmacht soldiers in US uniform captured during the Battle of the Bulge; seventeen were executed during the war.

Latchmere House, commonly called The Cage, for interrogating enemy prisoners.

Nuremberg War Crimes Tribunal. Many of the Nazi criminals escaped justice and some Nazi scientists were paid well to work in the USA. (*Yad Vashem archives*)

Vasily Grossman, the most famous Soviet journalist during the Second World War.

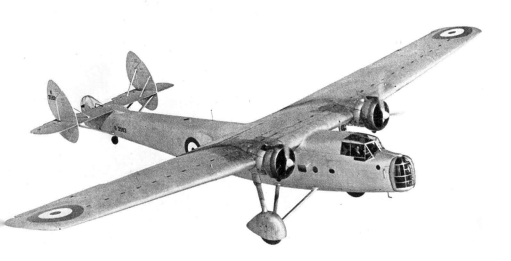

Bristol Bombays were used by the RAF to transport casualties as well as insert special forces. The Bombay was also used as a medium bomber. (*BAE Systems*)

Bernard Montgomery was almost the British answer to the German PR about Rommel.

30 June 1948. The picture shows the United Kingdom handing the port of Haifa over to the Israel Defence Force, with naval officers raising the flags of Israel and the Israeli Navy for the first time in the port. Prime Minister David Ben-Gurion is seen at left. (*IDF*)

Guy Stern reckoned that half of his PoWs were fanatical Nazis, 20 per cent were followers (until Hitler started losing); among the other 30 per cent were decent Germans. Some of these became trusties, deployed as stool pigeons in the temporary cages and then prison camps or used by the Ritchie Boys to help, perhaps with taking down notes from interrogations or in some cases translating German short-hand documents that were sometimes captured.

The Americans also had to adapt to the treatment of supposed collaborators in the rapidly expanding liberated parts of Europe. Some of the French-speaking Ritchie Boys were especially concerned that so many suspected collaborators were being shot out of hand and women frequently had their hair shaved off for allegedly consorting with German soldiers. Many of the French, punished by their own neighbours, may well have been guilty of heavy-duty collaboration but sometimes petty personal vendettas were worked out. Although many proud resistance fighters from the early period had survived, the American intelligence specialists were shocked at how many French people claimed allegiance to the Resistance, at the last minute. Clearly the French were exhibiting a collective guilty conscience not just about how quickly their very large army had been crushed but also how badly many of their private citizens and political leaders had behaved, not least to the Jews in France.

The British at the time were grateful for nature's gift of that very large anti-tank ditch, the English Channel. The Channel Islands, just off the coast of France, were the only part of the British Isles to be occupied. Perhaps if the mainland of Great Britain had been seized after Dunkirk, then the British may have behaved like the Channel Islanders and the French: 10 per cent active in the Resistance and 10 per cent active collaborators while the silent majority of the population tried to keep their heads down and their larders stocked.

The interrogators were active during the Battle of the Bulge when the deployment by the Wehrmacht of Germans in US uniform caused a few very tough encounters for the real Germans in real American uniforms. Circumstances had sometimes been difficult for the Ritchie Boys in the fight for the bridges around Arnhem when the Wehrmacht recaptured ground from the Allies, although most of the opposing troops were British.

For the Ritchie Boys the work was relentless. Once in a while, the lengthy daily intelligence reports were jazzed up by a harmless sexy story allegedly revealed during interrogation. But the humour went wrong when 'Hitler's latrine orderly' was supposedly interrogated. It went straight up to top intelligence people in Washington who were working on the Führer's psychology. A group of high-ranking intelligence experts were about to fly over to France until the Ritchie Boys got a supportive senior fighting general, who had appreciated the occasional humour in the many often dreary intelligence reports, to cover for them.

Two of the German Ritchie Boys also managed to attend a Marlene Dietrich concert for the front-line entertainment. They went backstage and their immaculate German won the attention of the most famous German actress-singer in the world. Once they told her what they did, she asked to visit their nearby camp. She went past the German PoWs in the cage who almost rioted with excitement when they saw the singer. She had to be escorted hastily from the premises.

Going home to *Deutschland*

When the Allied forces crossed the Rhine into Germany itself there were many surprises in store. For starters, they were amazed to find comfortable farmers and village homes with well-stocked larders, unlike the starvation they had seen in Holland. Sometimes the Germans fought hard on home soil and at other times they surrendered in their droves, eager to become prisoners of the benevolent Yankees. For the Ritchie Boys it was bitter-sweet to return to the land from which many had been forced to leave. The *leitmotif* was always finding one's family or at least news of them. Many had received no letters for years. A few Ritchie Boys had got word of their relatives who had fled to Holland before 1939. In a rare case or two, relatives had been found, emaciated and pale, after being hidden for years in the homes of brave Dutch men and women.

The biggest psychological sledgehammer was the discovery of the concentration camps. They had been talked about, but the stories were almost too dreadful to believe. Some Jewish resistance leaders in the east had passed information to the Americans via the Red Cross in Switzerland, begging the Allies to bomb places such as Auschwitz. But no deliberate bombing of camps took place until the last weeks of the war.

Buchenwald stood in a forest of beech trees which gave the forest its name. It was just a few miles from Weimar, where German democracy had briefly flowered after the Great War. Weimar was the centre of the German Enlightenment and the home of Johan Wolfgang von Goethe as well as Franz Liszt and Friedrich Schiller. In tragic cultural contrast, Buchenwald was the site of extermination through labour: *Vernichtung durch Arbeit*. At the very beginning of April 1945 Sergeant Herbert Gottschalk and another Ritchie Boy, Stephan Lewy, were among the first to reach the camp.

The US army found around 20,000 survivors on the first day of liberation. This included 3,800 Russians, 3,800 Poles, 2,900 French, 2,100 Czechs, 1,800 Germans and 1,200 Hungarians. There were also 4,000 Jews just about alive. In addition, the camp held, temporarily, 168 Allied PoWs.

Stephan Lewy immediately spoke to a Jewish survivor who explained that the prisoners were segregated by their nationality and the colour of their triangular patches, called a *Winkel* on their striped jackets. Yellow was for Jews, red for communists, black for Gypsies, pink for homosexuals; they all had their own separate barrack blocks.

The Ritchie Boys were tasked by senior US officers to order locals from nearby villages and Weimar to be forced to visit the site of so much horror. They were also told to find 100 male 'volunteers' a day to assist with the burials. Although elsewhere the former guards were often forced to deal with all the dead bodies, here the locals pitched up and many seemed genuinely shocked. '*Wir wussten nicht*' (We didn't know.) '*Niemand sagte uns*' (No one told us). And if they were interrogated, they would always say. '*Ich bin kein Nazi* – I am not a Nazi.' On the eve of the war, it was often hard to find a non-Nazi in Germany and suddenly in April 1945 nobody admitted to supporting Hitler.

When the Ritchie Boys interviewed the guards at various camps, they all claimed to be lowly functionaries just following orders. Very few ever showed any signs of a bad conscience.

When one of the local Germans started complaining about dragging corpses to the burial pits, he said: '*Der Geruch is schrecklich* – the smell is awful,' Stephan Lewy thought, but did not say, 'Breathe deep you bastard: it is your blind obedience to authority that caused this.'

Billy Wilder made a documentary film partly based on the Buchenwald experience, *Death Mills*. The film, originally in German, was made to educate the defeated country on what the Nazis had done in its name. There was also an English version. Wilder, although of Polish Jewish extraction, did not at all exaggerate the Jewish suffering. Ironically, history remembers not his powerful exposé of the camps but the comedic fluffiness of his Marilyn Monroe films such as *Some like it hot* and *Seven-Year Itch*.

Many Ritchie Boys hoped they might find their families in the camps. Guy Stern, for example, prayed that he might be re-united with his parents. 'But what he saw at Buchenwald ripped at his heart and took away what hope remained.'[6]

The Ritchie Boys were naturally involved in the de-Nazification programme. The Germans, being efficient and bureaucratic, often had extant lists of all the local Nazi leaders in the district police stations. The Germans in US uniforms admitted to enjoying putting the Nazi families through some of the tensions endured by the Jews in 1933–43 when they waited to be rounded up. The word soon spread in the smaller towns and Nazi functionaries would often be waiting with their small suitcases for the knock on the door. Nearly all the functionaries were not held for too long; they were often needed to repair and run electricity, sewage and water supplies in destroyed towns. Only the most senior Nazis were put on trial and then executed or jailed.

After the war many Ritchie Boys became famous. Some suffered immediately, however, from what is now called post-traumatic stress disorder. Staff Sergeant J.D. Salinger had entered Dachau in April 1945. That was perhaps the last straw after five tough campaigns, and he was hospitalised for a few weeks. Salinger later told his daughter, 'You never really get the smell of burning flesh out of your nose entirely, no matter how long you live.' He recovered sufficiently to volunteer for six-months of de-Nazification duties. A number of Salinger's biographers suggested that his writing was influenced by his wartime traumas. For example, 'For Esmé – with Love and Squalor' is a story narrated by a traumatized soldier. Salinger wrote to Ernest Hemingway in July 1946 and said that their chats in Paris were his few positive memories of the war.

Many Ritchie Boys never returned to Europe although one did retire to Berlin in 1988 and spent his final years visiting German schools to talk about his childhood under Hitler. Another Ritchie Boy was Hans Habe, a Hungarian, with a colourful past, including a spell in the French Foreign Legion as well as the US Army. He was tasked with setting up eighteen newspapers in the American zone of occupation. He later became a well-known journalist and author, with many pseudonyms and almost as many wives. And Richard Schifter was an Austrian who became an assistant secretary of state under both Ronald Reagan and George H.W. Bush.

German PoWs in the USA

Few Allied prisoners in PoW camps in the Reich wanted to settle in those lands, whereas up to 74 per cent of German prisoners in America left with very favourable opinions of their 'hosts' and indeed many wanted to stay in the USA. On 23 July 1946 the internment of 375,000 German PoWs and 60,000 Italian and Japanese PoWs was over.[7] The Americans had a justified reputation for humane treatment and that is why their millions of safe conduct passes were believed when they were air-dropped over areas held by the Wehrmacht at the end of the war; many thousands of German troops disbelieved the horror stories their officers told them and so surrendered to the Allies, especially the Americans, thus accelerating the Allied victory. Whether the US treatment of PoWs in the US and during immediate capture/surrender made the German treatment of their American prisoners any better has long been debated. The American infantry forces in the frontline were more likely, however, to shoot surrendering Wehrmacht than their British or Canadian counterparts. The Hitler Order to kill special forces and commandos has been to the fore but the question of whether US commitment to the Geneva Convention was fully reciprocated by Germany in their treatment of run-of-the-mill prisoners has not been answered and probably never will be.

The USA had to improvise to contain so many German troops in the 511 PoW camps it had established in America; some were high school gyms and even local fairgrounds. The Santa Anita racetrack, for example, was used as a temporary holding area for the thousands of Germans captured in North Africa. The Americans had to struggle with a number of PR disasters ranging from Nazism in the camps, big celebrations of Hitler's birthday, PoW kangaroo courts resulting in prisoner murders and the inevitable escapes. The senior military considered deploying a German Volunteer Corps to fight not the Russians but the Japanese. Yet hundreds of thousands of Germans worked on farms and in factories to alleviate the diversion of so many able-bodied American men who were fighting abroad. One of the most ironic jobs was a German PoW contract to work at a kosher meat-packing firm in New Jersey. Some right-wing guards helped several of their charges to escape, briefly, to Mexico while another guard machine-gunned to death eight Nazis in his charge after seeing a film on the Holocaust.

VIP Prisoners

British Nazi hunters in immediate post-war Europe were often driven to distraction by the Americans hiding, protecting and then employing key Nazis. Operation PAPERCLIP was largely run by the US Army's Counter Intelligence Corps who helped relocate around 1,600 Nazi engineers, scientists and technicians to the US; that figure does not include families. The Allies had already set up T-Force which looked for rocket data, and new designs in armoured vehicles and naval equipment, plus projects such as synthetic rubber.

The Nazis had a list of scientists who had been rehabilitated from dubious security levels to work on secret projects in the final years: the Osenberg list. The initial intention of US intelligence was not necessarily to grab research to fight the Red Army; of more immediate concern was the continuing war against Japan and then the possibility of German scientists moving to Spain, Egypt and Argentina, countries that had been generally sympathetic to Germany. But the Americans did initially focus on scientists and research centres in areas which they were scheduled to hand over to the USSR.

Many top German scientists were protected by the US forces and only one PAPERCLIP scientist, George Rickhey, was tried for war crimes and he was later acquitted in Germany.

'PO Box 1142' was the cover name for American military intelligence's two main prisoner projects. One looked at escape and evasion of US PoWs in Europe. The other, MIS-Y, was concerned with elite German prisoners. 'PO Box 1142' was started in 1942 and was based at Fort Hunt, Virginia, formerly part of George Washington's farmlands. Notable prisoners who were guests at this rural facility were Wernher von Braun, spymaster Reinhard Gehlen and Heinz Schlicke, an inventor of infra-red detection (although that detection system was also used by the Allies in the last stages of the war). The camp broke some of the Geneva Convention rules because the Red Cross was not notified of the transfer or location of PoWs. No torture was used but they did deploy Ritchie Boy standard techniques such as threatening to hand over truculent prisoners to the Russians. Between 1942 and 1946 over 3,400 VIP prisoners were questioned by military interrogators at the camp, and much data was gleaned, especially on weapons systems.

In 1946 the 100 comfortable barracks and less comfortable watch towers were bulldozed and the files regarding the site were largely hidden for fifty years.

Conclusion

When Hitler first declared war, he did so in the name of Germany and all Germans, including the country's half-million Jewish citizens. In the First World War more than 100,000 Jewish Germans had fought for the Kaiser; 12,000 had died fighting on the Eastern and Western fronts. Many were highly decorated. Most considered themselves Germans first and Jews second. A decade or so later even Jewish holders of the Iron Cross could not escape beatings and even murder at the hands of the Nazis. Being Jewish became a race, a *lower* race, not a religion. Many of the Jews persecuted were practising Christians, some married to Nazi-designated 'Aryans'. Only Germans with four non-Jewish German grandparents were deemed 'racially acceptable'. It was irrelevant whether they were practising Jews or practising Christians. By law, if you possessed 'Jewish blood' you were Jewish.

Why did Hitler hate Jews so passionately? Some have tried to explain his social environment: his failures as a painter and so on but the vast majority of people from Linz or Vienna did not become mad anti-Semites or at least manic enough to kill six million. The historian Ian Kershaw wrote a monumental biography of the Nazi warlord, in which he concluded: 'In truth we do not know for certain why, nor even when, Hitler turned into a maniac and obsessive anti-Semite.' Clearly, in the early 1920s when he wrote his autobiographic *Mein Kampf*, his paranoia about the Jews, especially based upon the forgery of *The Protocols of the Elders of Zion*, was already raging through his brain.[8]

This demonisation of the Jews perhaps cost Hitler the war. It was not just the massive amounts of manpower and money spent on the genocide of six million Jews and the exterminations enforced right to the last day of the war in Europe. It was not just the loss of German-Jewish scientific know-how, most notably in the race to produce the atomic bomb and some of the so-called wonder weapons. It was not just the moral stain that was to blight Germans for generations. In the specific case of the German-speaking Jewish Ritchie Boys, it was their passionate determination to strike back against Nazism that led to amazing intelligence gathering, both at tactical and operational levels. British intelligence experts would surely disagree, but the Americans claimed that approximately 60 per cent of credible intelligence gathered in Europe came from the Ritchie Boys. They saved many American lives on the front and perhaps shortened the war by six months.

Chapter Six

And They Also Served …

The Jewish Brigade

The Brigade, also called the Jewish Infantry Brigade, was formed in late 1944 mainly from Palestinian Jews, and mostly *sabras*, and was commanded mainly by Jewish officers from the British Army. The Brigade fought bravely in Italy and later was involved in all sorts of unauthorised killings of senior Nazis while also helping Jewish refugees, especially orphans, to get to Palestine. It was formally disbanded in 1946.

Palestinian Jewish authorities had long campaigned for a purely Jewish military unit within the British Army. Volunteers were eventually allowed to join, in equal numbers with Arab volunteers, in the Royal Army Service Corps and the Pioneer Corps. In 1942 the Palestine Regiment was formed, again with a supposedly equal number of largely unwilling Arabs. They were used for guarding prisoners in Egypt, but not in combat. The Yishuv authorities in Palestine still wanted a proper combat-worthy all-Jewish force.

Churchill had been a zealous promoter of Jewish combat-ready *German-speaking special forces* but was not keen to allow a Jewish army in the Mandate, not least because he thought it could be used against imperial forces. Official opinion in Whitehall and in Jerusalem was hostile. 'The British government knew they were dealing with men who had fought against them in the past, and very likely would be their enemies in the future.'[1] Nearly all of the Yishuv authorities and most of the illegal underground militias had, however, decided to fight *alongside* not *against* the British Mandatory government during the anti-Hitler war.

Eventually, Winston Churchill began to change his mind, partly because of the ever-increasing mountain of evidence of the Holocaust abominations, and partly to maintain the support of American opinion. He also realised that if he waited too long, it would be too late for a Jewish Brigade to fight the Nazis. The British prime minister announced that he'd had enough of the 'the usual silly objections'. In a personal message to the American president, he argued that 'the Jews ... of all races have the right to strike at the Germans as a recognisable body'. President Roosevelt replied that he had no objection.

In the House of Commons Churchill declared:

There are vast numbers of Jews serving with our forces, the American armies, and throughout all armies. It seems appropriate that a special Jewish unit of a race that has suffered indescribable torments from the Nazis should be represented as a distinct formation...

On Rosh Hashanah, 19 September 1944, the War Office announced that an infantry brigade would be based on the Jewish battalions of the Palestine Regiment. US and British newspapers said it was belated tokenism and a 'symbolic recognition' as the London *Times* put it. The *Manchester Guardian* opined that it was five years late. Some critics did offer the positive view that 'the British government has scored a victory over anti-Semitic prejudices'. Five thousand Jewish troops would be sent from Palestine to fight in Europe but again critics assumed the war would be over before they were engaged in combat.

The Brigade and its HQ was established in Egypt. Three infantry battalions were stood up with various support units including 200th Field Regiment of the Royal Artillery. The British hand-picked the Jewish and non-Jewish officers, while the new commander was considered to be a safe pair of hands: Brigadier Ernest Frank Benjamin. Born in Toronto, Benjamin had been in the army since 1919. Made a major in July 1943, he was Mentioned in Despatches for distinguished service in the Madagascar campaign of 1942. Some historians have even argued that the British-led capture of Vichy-controlled Madagascar before it could fall into Japanese hands was so crucial in the context of the war that it led to Japan's eventual downfall and defeat.

In October 1944 Benjamin led his men in a very stormy sea crossing from Alexandria to Italy. The brigade commander looked with pride on his Jewish soldiers with their golden star of David on their blue shoulder patches and announced to his officers that this was 'the first official Jewish fighting force since the fall of Judea to the Roman legions'. The Brigade joined Eighth Army in the Italian campaign in November.

The Brigade took up front-line combat positions for the Spring Offensive (Operation BUCKLAND) on 3 March 1945 along the south bank of the Senio River. The Jewish soldiers immediately began small-scale probing patrols against 42nd Jäger Division and 362nd Infantry Division of the Wehrmacht. The Jewish patrols fought hard and captured German prisoners. They also took on the German 4th Fallschirmjäger Division. The men from Palestine continued to excel in the river battles as its engineering units also assisted in bridging the Po River. On 23 March the Brigade relieved the 43 Gurkha Brigade for three days. Altogether the Brigade fought for forty-eight days in front-line combat in Italy.

Awards to the Brigade included: Military Cross x 4; Military Medal x 7; MBE x 4; OBE x 2; CBE x 1; Mention in Despatches x 78. In addition, 2 US awards were made. Mark Clark, then commander 15th Army Group, sent Brigade HQ a message:

> We are delighted to have the Jewish Brigade operating with our forces on the Italian Front. I wish the Brigade all the luck and success. I am greatly satisfied that the Jewish people who suffered so terribly at the hands of the Nazis should now be represented by this front line fighting force.

The Commander of the British X Corps wrote thus of the Brigade's performance: 'The Jewish Brigade fought well, and its men were eager to make contact with the enemy by any means available to them. Their staff work, their commands and their assessments were good.' On the other hand, the Brigade was accused of killing some surrendering German troops, especially members of the SS. No Brigade soldier, however, was ever punished for killing or mistreating German prisoners. Their commander had strongly empathised with their desire for revenge but he also emphasised that intelligence gained from German PoWs would hasten the end of the war and save many of those interned.

The Brigade moved north of the Po and then, in July 1945, to Belgium and the Netherlands. And then, finally, the German speakers 'came home' to serve in the British Army of the Rhine. The Jewish Brigade was disbanded in the summer of 1946 after eighty-three of its members had been killed in action or died of wounds. Many Brigade leaders became high-ranking officers in the Israel Defence Forces while men such as Israel Carmi became household names in the new Jewish state.

The Brigade also saved many Holocaust victims by working hand in glove with the *Bricha* (also *Bericha*) Movement and the Haganah to send as many as perhaps 20,000 Jewish survivors to Palestine. The American Jewish Joint Distribution Committee funded these clandestine operations. Anti-Semitism did not end with the death of Adolf Hitler; pogroms against Jews continued in the years after 1945, especially in eastern Europe. Most German and Austrian survivors did not expect to be able to return home.

Some members of the Jewish Brigade, sometimes with official British connivance, joined with Holocaust survivors to hunt down perpetrators of atrocities against Jews, particularly former members of the SS. Perhaps as many as 1,500 Nazi perpetrators were killed without judicial process.

In the Air

One of the founding fathers of Jewish heroes in the air was Wing Commander Lionel Frederick William Cohen DSO MC (First World War) DFC (Second World War). Born in Newcastle, he went on to enjoy an adventurous time in southern Africa. When the Second World War broke out, Cohen was 64 years old but he still managed to secure a commission as a pilot officer in the RAF and began service in Coastal Command in what was his fourth war. Air Marshal Sir John Slessor, when recommending Cohen for his DFC, wrote that 'few, if any, commanders can have had a junior officer with a campaign medal (Matabeleland) won before the CO was born!'² Cohen had also served in the Boer War and one obituary noted that he had served in all three armed services, earning the nickname as 'the man with a hundred lives'.

Cyril Stanley Bamberger, usually known to his friends as 'Bam', was born into a Jewish family in Cheshire and joined the Auxiliary Air Force. He was later accepted for pilot training with the Royal Air Force Volunteer Reserve in 1938. When the war started, he was flying Spitfires out of Biggin Hill and fought in No. 610 Squadron after the Dunkirk evacuation. He was credited with a 'probable' downing of a Messerschmitt Bf 109 in August 1940 off the Kent coast. In October he got his first confirmed combat victory of a Bf 109 over Canterbury. 'Bam' volunteered for the highly dangerous task of defending Malta where he shot down two Junkers Ju 87s over Grand Harbour in January 1941. After service in North Africa, he was commissioned and returned to Malta where he was awarded the DFC. After a brief post-war retirement, he returned to No. 610 Squadron as its CO in 1950 for the Korean War while converting to the Gloster Meteor. He later served in intelligence in the Air Ministry and was promoted to squadron leader. Bamberger was awarded a Bar to his DFC. Before retiring from the RAF in 1959, he converted to flying helicopters and served in Aden.

Among the Few

The Battle of Britain in 1940 was a fight for air supremacy, without which the Germans could not risk invading the main islands of Britain. Hitler's Operation SEALION was delayed and delayed again and then the intensity of the war in Russia meant that Britain was not to suffer the same fate as France. Although Jews in the RAF served in disproportionately large numbers compared with the general Jewish population in the UK, their numerical contribution was reduced but not just because of traditional anti-Semitism. Most of the British pilots were originally pre-war regular officers or NCOs and some of those were weekend fliers who had learned to fly privately or in university air squadrons. Like many exclusive clubs, the pilot class was a self-selecting white male middle-class group that tended to exclude Jews. This was true of the large Polish contingent as well as the colonial fliers. Many pilots, especially in the Polish force, changed their names and hid their religion because of both Polish anti-Semitism and obvious German hostility if they were to be captured.[3] This was just one difficulty in determining precise figures.

Frank Samuel Deitchman, who changed his surname to Day, was born in Hackney but grew up in the more prosperous, largely Jewish suburb of Golders Green. His father was an eminent theatrical agent. Day was a successful journalist but he enlisted in the RAF Volunteer Reserve the day Germany invaded Poland. He was a sergeant observer who flew with No. 248 Squadron in the Bristol Blenheim IVF fighter variant on initially anti-shipping raids, convoy escort and recce missions. He was commissioned and later was injured so badly that he became one of the famous 'guinea pigs' for Sir Archibald McIndoe, the brilliant plastic surgeon from New Zealand. Unfortunately, Day was killed in action in July 1942, aged 28, while flying to Malta.

One of the 'aces' (a pilot with five confirmed kills) was Flying Officer George Ernest Goodman, often called Benny after the band leader. He was a *Sabra*, born in Haifa, but was sent to school in Highgate, London. He joined the Officers Training Corps while at school and later served in a Hurricane squadron. Credited with ten planes shot down and six others in shared attacks, he fought in the Battle of France, the Battle of Britain and then in the Desert campaigns. After earning the DFC, he was shot down by flak over Gazala in Libya in June 1941.

The youngest Jewish RAF man killed was Norman Jacobson from Grimsby who was a radio operator with No. 29 Squadron, but in August 1940 his Blenheim was shot down and all the crew were killed. Jacobson was just 18. Many of the young Jewish pilots were killed in the Battle of Britain.

Of the 145 Poles flying in the RAF a number were Jews. Zygmunt 'Joe' Klein was a sergeant pilot who fought against the Luftwaffe in 1939–40. He escaped to Britain via France and joined the RAF in February 1940 and was considered one of the bravest Spitfire aviators. The Poles were determined to kill Germans as well as shoot down their planes. They hated the Nazis with real intensity. He crashed landed and baled out a number of times, as well as shooting down the enemy. Klein went missing in action flying above the Isle of Wight, probably brought down by Bf.109s. He was awarded the Polish Cross of Valour and Bar.

Herbert Ronald Sharman was a squadron leader who participated in SOE operations; with No. 297 Squadron which specialised in inserting agents into occupied Europe. They used the Armstrong Whitworth Whitley, a medium bomber, with five crew. Later he flew VIPs to summit meeting such as Casablanca and Yalta. Sharman was awarded the AFC just after the end of the war.

William Henry Nelson was a Canadian who flew with No. 24 Squadron. He had joined the RAF in 1937 and took part in the initial bombing raids during the Dunkirk evacuation. When the King presented him with his DFC at Buckingham Palace on 4 June 1940, he became the first Canadian Jew to be decorated in the Second World War. He wrote a letter home which said: 'Thank God I shall be able to help destroy the regime that persecutes Jews.'⁴ A few months later he was killed in action, at just 23, leaving behind a wife and young son.

Wing Commander Robert Roland 'Lucky' Tuck was one of the most decorated Jewish aces with thirty kills. He was shot down four times, was wounded twice, collided twice and both baled out and crash-landed in the Channel. In January 1942 he was shot down by flak outside Boulogne while on a low-level strafing operation. Because of his reputation he was interviewed by the German ace, Adolf Galland; after the war, and ironically for a Jewish pilot, he was made an honorary member of Galland's former squadron. He helped plan the famous 'Great Escape' from Stalag Luft III but was moved before he could take part. Unlike many of his contemporaries, Lucky Tuck's luck did not run out because he managed his full span of three score and ten.

Bomber Command

Jews flew in bombers as well as fighters. Special Duty Operators in No. 101 Squadron of Bomber Command needed to be German speakers and many Jewish airmen filled the role. The Germans deployed a complex system to co-ordinate their fighters to counter RAF and US bombers.

A British system called ABC (Airborne Cigar) used a receiver and three transmitters on the German VHF frequency and would jam the ground controllers' signals. Lancasters added an eighth crew man in a special conversion for the radio-jamming role. The Special Duty Operators or SOs would be in triple danger: bomber crews had the highest casualty rate (and SOs the highest) plus they were usually German, and they were Jewish. Because the ABC planes were spread throughout the bomber stream and used on nearly all missions, the casualty rate was the highest in the RAF. If the SOs were captured, they would be treated mercilessly by the Gestapo. The ABC system became operational and successful from September 1943. The Germans soon caught on and started to target the modified bombers although the Lancasters were visually distinguishable only by two seven-foot aerials on top of the fuselage. The Germans were probably able to monitor the ABC transmissions and so vector their fighters against the special Lancasters. During the war both sides played cat and mouse with new counter and counter-counter-measure methods. The Germans referred to the initial ABC system as '*dudelsack*' – the German for bagpipes because of the warbling sound.

German-speaking – mainly Jewish – RAF men and WAAF women also worked in listening and broadcasting stations in England in what was called the Corona system. They sometimes could break into the fighter-controllers' frequencies and issue confusing orders – perhaps to make emergency landings or warn of non-existent fog.

Sailors

Three Jews were awarded the Victoria Cross in the Second World War. Tommy Gould was one of them. He was a petty officer on board the submarine HMS *Thrasher*. In February 1942, north of Crete, the submarine was attacked by aerial bombing and depth charges. Two of the bombs were lodged unexploded in the sub. One was removed fairly easily but Gould with one other sailor entered a space of not more than two feet in height to remove the other. It took fifty minutes to drag – very slowly – the loudly ticking device and then it was thrown overboard. Gould was also a member of the 43 Group, an association of Jewish ex-servicemen who fought fascists in the UK after the war.

During the Second World War over 2,000 British Jews served in the Royal Navy and Royal Marines plus around 300 Jewish women served in the WRNS while many more served in the Merchant Navy. Over 200 Jews in the RN were killed in action.

One of the least-known operations of the Second World War took place in May 1941. Operation BOATSWAIN was one of the first joint missions between the *Palmach* and the British. The British sought to attack Vichy French forces in Lebanon and Syria. The targets chosen were the oil installations in Tripoli, Lebanon, that were heavily defended by Senegalese troops in the French Vichy army. A British SOE officer, Major Sir Anthony Palmer, and twenty-three *Palmach* commandos left Haifa on a police launch on 18 May 1941 – and were never seen again. Later, a commission of enquiry suggested that they might have been the victims of a submarine attack or the accidental detonation of the explosives they were carrying. Another version has the commandos landing in Tripoli but being intercepted and destroyed. The *Palmach* was alleged to have hushed up the disaster to maintain morale at a fragile time.

Yank Levy

Bert 'Yank' Levy was a character conjured up out of the most extravagant Hollywood adventure films. He served with irregular forces around the world and took part in various conflicts including the Spanish Civil War. For British military history perspectives, he was active in the Osterley Park training school for the Home Guard during the Second World War. He was born into a large Jewish family in Hamilton, Canada, which subsequently moved to New York. Poorly educated, he studied, he always said, 'in the school of hard knocks' – literally because he became a boxer.

In 1916 he joined the British Merchant Marine as a stoker and later he enrolled in the Jewish Legion. He claimed to have become a devotee of guerrilla warfare after talking to some of Lawrence of Arabia's scouts while serving in the Jordan valley with the Legion. The British had taught the itinerant adventurer the joys of the Lewis machine gun, a skill he used in various wars. After serving six years in jail in the USA for armed robbery, he was deported back to Canada. Some of Yank Levy's biography was embellished by himself, although the original true core remains impressive. Probably. He apparently deployed his machine-gun skills in Nicaragua while indulging in gun-running. Levy was also said to have been involved in training the Mexican army. Yank Levy did serve in the British Battalion of the International Brigade in the Spanish Civil War. He was captured by the Fascists at the Battle of Jarama near Madrid where he had (briefly) deployed a heavy machine gun. After six months in a Francoist jail, he was released in a prisoner exchange for two officers. 'A fair exchange,' he said at the time; and then he went back to Canada to recruit volunteers for the Republican cause.

When the Second World War broke out, Levy tried and failed to join the Canadian army, probably because of his bad reputation and jail time. He teamed up with some former members of the British Battalion of the International Brigade in England, where he met up with the former battalion commander, Tom Wintringham, a Marxist journalist turned soldier. At Osterley Park in north London, Levy was involved in what became the unofficial training ground for defence volunteers who morphed into the Home Guard, originally set up to defend Britain from a fascist invasion.[5] The training school became famous because it was shown in cinema newsreels. While lecturing there, Wintringham helped Levy to write his famous book, *Guerrilla Warfare*, his practical guide. Levy did not have commando training but he nevertheless specialised in knife fighting and hand-to-hand combat. Churchill and the establishment never liked the school, partly because of the socialism preached there, so the War Office took it over and closed it in 1941. Many of the practical courses taught there were taken up by what became the Home Guard, however, and Levy's book was printed in a number of mass-market editions. Levy liked to compare his combat principles with historical figures, such as Hereward the Wake, but also used recent examples of resistance such as those espoused by both Colonel T.E. Lawrence and Orde Wingate. *Time* magazine noted at the time: 'Anyone who thinks this country [UK] will be invaded – which includes anyone now alive – would do well to read "Yank" Levy's *Guerrilla Warfare* for instruction to harass invaders.'

Despite his previous incarceration, Levy's reputation was such that he was invited back to the US to teach partisan warfare both to the regular army and the National Guard, which was becoming more relevant after Germany invaded Russia and large partisan bands proliferated behind Nazi lines. Levy spent time in Canada proselytising about his methods, while he also designed and tried, unsuccessfully, to market a combat knife. The veteran campaigner was distrusted in the UK because of his communist and socialist connections since his time in Spain although Levy lectured extensively in the US and was billed as an instructor in 'cad warfare to the British commandos'. The now aging commando was a clever self-publicist, promoting himself by saying that Goebbels had promised that he would be 'the first to be shot when the Germans captured England'. Considered to be a major Jewish war hero by a number of Jewish organisations, his attempt to go to Palestine in 1946 failed because of US passport 'problems'. Nevertheless, Levy was pardoned for his 1927 conviction for armed robbery, not least because of his war record. The arch-adventurer was now broke and sick. He died of a heart attack in 1965.

Bletchley Park

Jewish intellectual and linguistic skills played a vital role in codebreaking at Bletchley Park and in other 'out-stations'. The intelligence centre was roughly halfway between Oxford and Cambridge and also close to London but rural enough to avoid being involved in urban bombing campaigns. Ironically, the 55-acre estate, before it was bought by the government, was the Victorian home of the Anglo-Jewish banking family of Sir Herbert and Lady Fanny Leon. Churchill was passionately involved in the work of the codebreakers and had their latest data hand-delivered almost daily. Initially it was charged with decoding German military signals often via the Enigma machine; other machines and codes were cracked later. Finally, the Americans came on board and worked on Japanese codes.

Just one example was Professor Peter John Hilton from North London. He was grabbed by the Intelligence services when he was just 18 while studying maths at Oxford and had only basic German. He worked under Major Ralph Tester in the so-called 'Testery' at Bletchley. Hilton worked with the codebreaking genius Alan Turing and Roy Jenkins (later Chancellor of the Exchequer) and also Peter Benenson (formerly Solomon), the Jewish founder of Amnesty International. They worked on specialist signals used for officers' eyes only and later the traffic between Hitler and senior generals that used a more complex machine than Enigma. Their work led to the creation of Colossus, the first programmable computer. Hilton and Turing became friends and Hilton defended Turing when he felt he was being forced into suicide in 1954 because of his homosexuality. Hilton shared the opinion of fellow Jewish codebreaker Jack Good that, if Turing had been driven to suicide earlier, 'We might have lost the war'.

Technically called the Government Code and Cypher School, the inmates joked that it was the Golf, Cheese and Chess Society. More commonly it was called Station X and always 'BP' by inmates, who often kept their secrets until death. Initially the experts were mostly men but soon numerous female linguists, academics and crossword specialists joined and then the place was derided as 'Boffins and Debs' by the few in the know in Whitehall. Many were German-speaking Jews or English-speaking Jewish academics who became involved with cracking mainly German codes, but also Italian and Soviet signals (there was also a station monitoring the Soviets based in Sarafand in Palestine). Roughly 10,000 experts passed through BP, although the average complement at any one time was 7,000 to 8,000; many became burnt out because of the intensity of the work and long shifts. Most intelligence experts would agree that the work done there probably shortened the war by two to four years. Or even prevented Britain losing outright early in the conflict.

The Secret Listeners

Trent Park, a stately home in North London, was possibly almost as important as Bletchley Park, although it is far less well known. Originally the home of Sir Philip Sassoon, a wealthy Iraqi Jew, it rather resembled a gentlemen's club, although the inmates were mostly captured senior German generals. The very senior officers had their own bedrooms with adjoining sitting rooms and there was a room for playing billiards and another for table tennis. A so-called Scottish aristocrat, Lord Aberfeldy, who also claimed to be a cousin of the king, was their liaison officer. The 'peer' would arrange for a Saville Row tailor to measure them for new suits and occasionally took them for tea at the Ritz. But no such title existed; it was a brilliant act by an MI6 officer. And, above all, Trent Park was wired for sound. From trees and plants to lamps and tables as well as many walls, all had listening devices. Even the billiard table had a bugging device. The whole thing was almost a theatrical stage set and none of the German top brass was suspicious. One of the prisoners, Lieutenant Colonel Kurt Kohncke, said: 'Our involuntary hosts are thoroughly gentlemanlike.'

Unseen by the PoW officers, an army of secret listeners (mainly German-speaking Jews from all over the Reich and conversant with the many dialects) were hidden behind the stage set. The conversations were transcribed, translated and carefully double-checked before being passed to interrogators and intelligence agencies. Trent Park had associated country houses in Latimer House and Wilton in the Buckinghamshire countryside although Trent Park tended to house the VIPs.

Most of the secret files were not declassified until the late 1990s. (The Americans also had numerous similar files and they had supplied the advanced bugging devices.) The eavesdropping, commonly called Operation M (for miked rooms), produced some amazing data. And not just on battlefield plans but also new technology, especially regarding Hitler's wonder weapons, such as the V1 and V2 programmes. The listeners also produced fascinating evidence of who supported and who opposed the July 1944 plot to kill Hitler. And there were graphic discussions about the mass murders of Jews in the East by the officers who had ordered and then implemented them.

Some junior officers were screened as well and often the interrogators played dumb. As Fritz Lustig, one of the secret Jewish listeners, noted long after the war: 'Their reaction to interrogation was often particularly fruitful. They would tell their cellmate what they had been asked about, what they had managed to conceal from the interrogator and how much we [the British] already knew.'[6]

The overall project came under the control of the Combined Services Detailed Interrogation Centre and was run by a remarkable long-term spook, Colonel Thomas Kendrick, who was a South African born in Cape Town and who had served with the British in the Boer war and as a field intelligence officer in the Great War. His MI6 cover in the Vienna embassy before the war was that of a passport officer called 'Colonel Wallace'. In her book, *The Walls Have Ears*, author Helen Fry dubs Kendrick the 'Oskar Schindler of Vienna' in that he finessed or outright forged papers to allow up to 200 Jews per day to escape. Later Kendrick did a deal with Adolf Eichmann to allow 1,000 Jews to emigrate to Palestine, even though he was reprimanded by the Foreign Office for this freelancing. After being arrested by the Gestapo and enduring four days of interrogation, Kendrick was forced out of Austria. Despite this, the spymaster always retained an affection for the German language and culture, perhaps encouraged by his German wife.

Kendrick also set up a specialist eavesdropping project for Rudolf Hess when the deputy Führer flew to Scotland in 1941. One of the major (spurious) conspiracy theories about this flight was that Hitler's deputy had flown over with a peace deal but Churchill had suppressed any mention of the offer. But Kendrick's major coup in the realm of secret projects was the crucial intelligence he gained in the so-called 'Battle of the Beams' when the various measures and countermeasures for radio navigation were being developed. His listeners also learned a great deal about U-boat movements and tactics in the Battle of the Atlantic, a war that Britain almost lost.

As the war turned in the Allies' favour, especially in North Africa, the number of prisoners began to swamp Kendrick's resources. And the answer was more Jewish refugees, enemy aliens, many still serving in the Pioneer Corps. By 1943 about 100 former enemy aliens were serving under Kendrick. The spymaster would tell his Jewish recruits that 'Your work here is as important as firing a gun in action.'

Some of the Jewish recruits were disguised as stool pigeons dressed in Wehrmacht uniforms. The acting and language skills were very demanding for the fifty or so Jews who volunteered. Although the centres were surrounded by guards, the PoWs could have inflicted serious damage if the undercover men were discovered.

The bugging centres collected massive amounts of intelligence about war crimes. When the war ended in Europe Kendrick forced the senior PoWs to watch films of Bergen-Belsen, Buchenwald and Dachau. One German general commented: 'We are disgraced for all time and 1,000 years will not wipe out what we've done.' Most senior PoWs were not contrite, however, often arguing that Russian treatment of Germans was worse. There were also lots of conspiracy theories discussed about Britain and America wanting to destroy the German military and return the former Reich to a purely agricultural society unable to wage modern war, which in reality was seriously discussed in the American Morgenthau plan. Mostly the Wehrmacht officers absolved themselves by blaming 'a few beasts in the SS'.

Kendrick was determined that his work would bring to justice those guilty of war crimes. The secret listeners preserved any relevant recordings, marking the acetate discs with a large 'A' for atrocity. The evidence, however, was not used at the Nuremberg trials because, with the Soviet threat looming, the British did not want to reveal their eavesdropping methods and so the secrets were stored away for fifty years. Although some critics derided the soft treatment of the generals as a 'Mad Hatter's Tea Party', it could be argued that without the secret listeners and the information they obtained, then it could have been London not Hiroshima that was devastated by the first atomic bomb.

Chapter Seven

Resistance

In what was the last political act of disgraced Prime Minister Neville Chamberlain, he signed the founding charter of the Special Operations Executive which was activated on 22 July 1940. The structure of the SOE was based on country sections and its HQ was at 64 Baker Street. Right from the start the SOE had a strong Jewish flavour. Besides the many gifted linguists, agents and cypher experts, Marks and Spencer donated the whole of their HQ's fifth floor at Baker Street for the duration of the war. And the first director was the Jewish banker, Sir Charles Hambro, a decorated veteran from the First World War. SOE had a number of outstations, the first being based in Cairo, in Rustum Buildings, known to every cab driver in the city as 'the secret house'.

Churchill, always an inveterate devotee of irregular warfare, was a dedicated supporter of the SOE. He swore that 'his' agents would 'set Europe ablaze'. Initially, however, the new organisation had little to work with, although by July 1942, like all bureaucracies, it had grown to comprise 2,000 members of staff in Britain and a further 600 in the Middle East.

Originally, the SOE thought that, perhaps with a bit of clever propaganda, inspiring leadership and a generous supply of ammunition, the subject nations of Europe would rise up. SOE believed that the most likely national insurrection would be in Poland. Many in the British establishment had a soft spot for the Poles; after all, Britain had gone to war because of the German invasion of Poland and the Polish pilots in the Battle of Britain were lionised. So SOE went out of its way to work with the two main Polish factions in London. In contrast, the Belgian government in exile was considered so cantankerous that SOE said it would not work with them. Inevitably the French were the most difficult.

To be fair, in 1940 no one knew if General Charles de Gaulle commanded any real support in France.

Poland was always an exception; it could be argued that the country had been in resistance since 1772. The readiness of other occupied countries to get rid of the Germans was something that varied sharply according to the state of the war. In the first traumatic shock of defeat and occupation most people submitted and struggled to stay alive. Not many occupied Europeans had much hope until Hitler invaded the USSR. And even the Czechs, once again occupied by German-speaking conquerors from 1939, could do little more than imitate the wonderful example of the good soldier Schweik, a highly successful resister, who appeared very affable and helpful to the Germans while doing everything wrong. Many French, Belgians and Danes were, in 1940–41, mostly fairly content to be part of the new order in Europe, so long as they could get enough to eat. Deep in the countryside there was rarely much trouble about that. Cynically, the resistance movements bloomed, after the imminent defeat of Germany became obvious to everybody except Hitler and a small coterie of fanatics. French opinion changed dramatically after D Day.

Meanwhile, SOE's recruitment changed from the pre-war intelligence modus operandi of asking dons which of their students were the 'right sort of chap' with the right sort of languages. For a start, many women were now recruited. They were considered more capable of acting alone and showing more determination and courage. Women were initially recruited from the WAAF (Women's Auxiliary Air Force) and FANY (First Aid Nursing Yeomanry). Motivations varied. The famous heroine Violette Szabo said she wanted revenge for her husband who was killed on active service; and Nancy Wake, a New Zealander living in Marseilles, joined up because she was disgusted by the treatment of Jews in Vienna after the *Anschluss*. Wake was one who managed to survive the war because of her exceptional ability to elude the Gestapo who called her 'the white mouse' because of her uncanny elusiveness.

Many would-be agents were trained in Scotland and some failed the initial course. One agent said after the war: 'SOE was looking for gangsters with the knowledge of gangsters but with the behaviour, if possible, of gentlemen.'[1] One operative recruited in Cairo was asked directly: 'Have you any personal objection to committing murder?' Although some of the more arduous instruction was done in Scotland, SOE took over so many stately homes in England (around fifty) that the organisation earned the nickname of 'Stately 'Omes of England'.

SOE had to deal with the quarrelsome European allies while also contending with the kaleidoscopic feuding of the German security systems. It faced as many rivals at home as it did in the campaign to liberate the continent. SOE was not part of the official war machine but rather came under the Ministry of Economic Warfare. Yet it had to work with the War Office to get planes and boats to take its people to the continent. The three armed services were very wary of the new secret organisation, however. But the main opponent was the Foreign Office. (Just as during the First Cold War, 1946–1991, the inmates of the British Ministry of Defence used to half-joke that their main enemy was not the USSR but the Foreign Office, so great was the rivalry and even outright hostility.) The biggest threat to SOE's survival was, however, SIS (Special Intelligence Service or, more commonly, MI6). The SOE-SIS nexus bore a resemblance to a fractious relationship between ex-spouses except that they were disputing the custody of countries, not children.

The relationship with the Americans was better; they copied the SOE with their Office of Strategic Services, OSS. It was run by a remarkable maverick of a man, 'Wild Bill' Donovan, a lawyer, diplomat and the only military officer to have been awarded the four highest US awards for bravery after serving in both world wars. The OSS faced similar turf wars as in the UK, especially with the Pentagon and State Department. But the OSS survived because of the ardent backing of President Roosevelt just as the SOE endured because of Churchill's persistent and obsessive interest in irregular warfare.

And yet Churchill did not step in to prevent the internecine turf wars. He could have ensured that the lines of demarcation between SIS, SOE, the Admiralty and Combined Operations were clearly defined. Either he was too busy or he thought the warring fiefdoms were more efficient in the end, because he liked playing favourites off against each other.

Churchill had been cautioned several times by senior officials. Sir Stewart Menzies, the head of SIS, warned the prime minister, who was of course also the defence minister, of the difficulties of what would follow 'when two sets of secret agents worked independently into the same territory'.

To take one example of how this maze of secrecy worked. In December 1939 a special sub-committee of the Joint Intelligence Committee met to discuss escaped British PoWs and recently downed airmen trying to evade capture. Present were the head of MI5 (Directorate of Military Intelligence, Section 5, cover name for the Security Service), MI6 (cover name for the Secret Intelligence Service) and the Naval Intelligence Division. The result of the meeting was the creation of MI9. This would be responsible for the return of escaping Allied troops (35,000 in all), although eighteen months later a new section, MI19, was set up to deal with the interrogation of enemy PoWs.

In the middle of all this, the SOE struggled for the first eighteen months but gradually the lights were slowly being switched on in the Nazi-imposed darkness. And the entry into the war by the USA and the USSR in 1941 offered many more opportunities for clandestine action.

Jewish resistance in Europe

Jews formed less than one per cent of the German population in 1933 and it was less than half a per cent when war broke out six years later. Organised resistance was extremely difficult. The communist party advised its members either to leave Germany or, if they could not do so, to form their own cells *outside* the communist underground. Small Jewish resistance groups, both Zionist and pro-communist, did survive until just before the war. One was the Herman Baum group in Berlin. Nearly all opposition was inevitably squashed by the Gestapo, so the Jewish groups in Germany achieved little during the war but in post-war East Germany the Baum group became a symbol of Jewish resistance and a Berlin street was named after Baum. More successful were the approximately 300 German Jews, mainly communists, who fought in the French Maquis. Some survived the war.

Explicitly Jewish partisan groups were formed within the French resistance; they were mainly Jews from eastern Europe. They attacked German units but not with the deliberate intention of preventing the Jewish deportations leaving for extermination camps, although a few minor attacks on deportation trains did happen. A much smaller group, *Armée Juive*, trained people to live in Palestine and later prepared them to join the Jewish Brigade. After D Day the small Jewish units combined to form the *Organisation Juive de Combat* (OJC) and they fought alongside the mainstream Maquis.

The Vichy French authorities followed German orders to register Jews for later deportation; in Poland it was the Jewish leadership itself that organised the registration. In the beginning, most seemed to believe that Jews were being sent to work, not extermination, camps. It seemed to take a long time to accept that the Germans were planning a 'final solution', proof yet again that people will usually believe what they want to believe. In Holland the Jewish leadership bargained for some Jews not to be deported; these were families of the Jewish authorities as well as key workers in the war industries and textile factories.

> This suited the German thinking perfectly: they had discovered from experience that as long as one group of Jews thought they were immune they would be willing to help remove another, saving the occupiers a great deal of manpower and effort as well as preserving the appearance of order.[2]

Facing the overwhelming power and terror of Nazi occupiers, the Jewish councils often had little option but to comply. It is very easy now to criticise the fact that many Jewish councils offered up some Jews in order to save other Jews, if only temporarily. The leader of the *Judenrat* (council) in Warsaw could not face the moral dilemma when he was ordered to send another 7,000 Jews the next day for deportation. Adam Czerniaków, the council leader, committed suicide rather than comply. A friend said that he 'may not have lived his life with honour but he did die with honour'. To say that Jews collaborated or co-operated with the Germans is a historical misrepresentation – they were coerced by German terror to submit and comply. Yet the charge remains that many Jewish leadership groups were more concerned with finessing Nazi orders rather than fostering resistance. Especially in the eastern ghettos, constant debates proliferated about if and when to rise up. When was the most appropriate time and would it lead to the immediate death of all the Jews involved?

It is also sometimes ignored by gentile historians that some Jews went willingly to their deaths on religious grounds. Generations of Jews have performed the religious act of *Kiddush Hashem*, the hallowing of God's name by deliberately accepting death rather than renounce Yahweh. Submitting to their deaths in gas chambers was a resistance of the spirit if not the body.[3] On the other hand, many religious Jews gave up on their God and claimed that He had died in camps such as Auschwitz and Belsen.

In occupied Europe there were many Christians who hid their Jewish friends and neighbours, and sometimes even strangers, from the German authorities. In Poland, however, the Nazi occupiers used to pay a bonus to locals who betrayed Jews, who were often 'double-dipping' by already blackmailing the same Jews whom they later denounced when all the money had been sucked out of them. In Holland about 60 per cent of the Jews who went into hiding, most notably Anne Frank and her family, were betrayed by collaborators – some of whom were Jews trying to save their own families, temporarily.

In contrast, many Jews fought back even in the dire conditions in the ghettoes and the camps. In the small hours of 19 April 1943 over 2,000 German troops with Ukrainian auxiliaries plus tanks and artillery began clearing the Warsaw ghetto. The date was special: 20 April was Hitler's birthday and Heinrich Himmler, the SS chieftain, wanted to offer him the ghetto's destruction as a little gift.

In the previous summer of 1942, around 250,000 Jews had been deported from the ghetto to be killed in Treblinka. Some of the remaining Jews began building bunkers and tunnels and smuggling in weapons and explosives. The left-wing Jewish Combat Organisation (ZOB) and the right-wing Jewish Military Union (ZZW) began to train and prepare themselves. The Germans ordered the burning of the ghetto, block by block, ending on 16 May 1943. A total of 12,000 Jews were killed, about half burnt alive or suffocated. The ghetto survivors were sent to Treblinka anyway. A few of the militant leaders escaped to the forests to join the partisans but most stayed to fight to the last man. German casualties were fewer than 150.

The Polish Home Army had helped the Jews by smuggling in some arms. One of their leaders said admiringly: 'Practically defenceless, they took to fighting without the slightest chance of success.' Other uprisings took place in extermination camps but Warsaw was the largest single revolt by Jews during the Second World War. (The city was also the site of the largest non-Jewish uprising: the Home Army's urban insurgency which lasted sixty-three days during the summer of 1944. The Red Army had reached the suburbs but did not, or could not, engage with the Wehrmacht, a subject of much historical debate.)

After the Warsaw ghetto was razed to the ground, some Jewish survivors fought with the partisans, because they wanted to live out their remaining days as free men and women, meeting death honourably. Jews were not always welcomed by the partisans, partly because of anti-Semitism, but also because Jews usually arrived with no weapons and no money, and their destitute nature earned them the reputation of bandits looting the peasants. Some fell in with the Red Army as it advanced but they were sometimes caught in the middle of fighting with the Polish and Ukrainian nationalists. Other Jewish groups formed their own independent fighting and family units.

Most of the resistance stories, especially in Poland, emphasise male Jewish fighters but recently the literature has turned to the feminist history of resistance. Judy Batalion's remarkable new book, *The Light of Days: Women Fighters of the Jewish Resistance*, examines how young Jewish women fought the Nazis mainly from their bases in the ghettoes:

> These 'ghetto girls' paid off Gestapo guards, hid revolvers in loaves of bread, and helped build systems of underground bunkers. They flirted with Nazis, bought them off with wine, whiskey and pastry

and, with stealth, shot and killed them. They carried out espionage missions for Moscow, distributed fake IDs and underground flyers, and were bearers of the truth about what was happening to the Jews. They helped the sick and taught the children; they bombed German train lines and blew up Vilna's electricity supply. They dressed up as non-Jews, worked as maids on the Aryan side of town, and helped Jews escape the ghettos through canals and chimneys, by digging holes in walls and crawling across rooftops. They bribed executioners, wrote underground radio bulletins, upheld group morale, negotiated with Polish landowners, tricked the Gestapo into carrying their luggage filled with weapons, initiated a group of anti-Nazi Nazis and, of course, took care of most of the underground's admin.[4]

Armed underground Jewish groups, male and female, operated in more than ninety eastern European ghettos. Uprisings took place in Warsaw as well as in Bedzin, Vilna, Bialystok, Kraków, Lvov, Częstochowa, Sosnowiec and Tarnów. Armed Jewish resistance broke out in at least five major concentration camps and death camps, including Auschwitz, as well as in eighteen forced labour camps. Over 30,000 Jews joined forest partisan detachments.

They all faced the similar dilemmas. They were few Jews with fewer guns and so they were not going to topple or even stop the Nazis for long, so what was the point of fighting back? Were they just fighting to die with dignity and perhaps create some kind of resistance legacy? Were they trying to save individual Jews, especially children, or save their respective political movements? Should the Jews fight in the ghettos or the forests? As Jews alone or with the Poles and later the Red Army?

Jews based in the UK

Jews were recruited in large numbers for a variety of reasons. They were often well-educated and many possessed a burning hatred of the Nazi regime. Many were recent immigrants into the UK, and knew the languages and current culture of their former countries well. They faced, as ever, the double jeopardy of being an SOE spy and Jewish. Most were given a new religion and regular military backgrounds. Often, even if their back stories held on capture, as SOE agents they were routinely tortured and murdered.

Many Jews worked on the fringes of the SOE, for example, in the special 'Moonlight' squadrons of the RAF or labouring for long hours as wireless operators in the Baker Street HQ. Often there were temporary attachments from and with, for example, the Small Scale Raiding Force or X Troop.

Haganah agents had cross-over roles – working for both the Yishuv and the British. One of the most famous later in Israel was Hannah Szenes (also Senesh; in Hebrew חנה סנש). Born in Budapest in 1921 and was murdered at 23, she was a gifted poet who embraced Zionism when she joined the *Maccabea*, a Hungarian student Zionist movement. She emigrated to Israel and joined Kibbutz Sdot Yam where she was recruited into the Haganah. In 1943 she was enlisted in the WAAF and then into the SOE and was sent to Egypt for parachute training. The Yishuv wanted to send Jewish parachutists behind the lines to assist the Allies and help Jewish survivors. It planned to create a special Jewish commando unit within the British Army and Szenes was one of thirty-seven selected out of 250 volunteers to be sent on active missions.[5]

She and two colleagues were parachuted into Yugoslavia in March 1944 partly to aid Hungarian Jews about to be sent to Auschwitz. Her colleagues called off the mission after they were informed that the Germans had already occupied Hungary. Szenes continued and was arrested at the border by Hungarian border forces. They immediately found her British military transmitter used to communicate with SOE and other partisans. In prison she was stripped naked, tied to a chair and then whipped and clubbed for three days. She lost many of her teeth and suffered internal injuries. Nevertheless, Szenes refused to give the codes for the transmitter, even when her mother was dragged into the prison and threatened with the same treatment. The temporary fascist Arrow Cross regime tried her for treason (as she was originally Hungarian) and she was executed by a firing squad on 7 November 1944 as the Red Army pushed deeper into the country. She had refused a blindfold and insisted on facing her executioners. Her remains were later taken to Israel, where her poems and diary were published; numerous books and plays have celebrated her short life. Szenes has sometimes been called the Joan of Arc of Israel and a kibbutz was named in her hour (Yad Hannah). In the National Military Cemetery overlooking Jerusalem stand the graves of the thirty-two Palestinian Jewish parachutists, members of the British forces, who were dropped into Nazi-occupied Balkan countries. Szenes is with them.

Szenes's story is not well-known outside Israel whereas some of the British Jewish SOE agents are reasonably well-publicised. Martin Sugarman lists Captain Adam Rabinovich, murdered by the Gestapo, Captain Isadore Newman, killed in Mauthausen, and Captain Maurice Pertschuck, murdered in Buchenwald.[6] Of the thirty-nine women inserted into France, fifteen were captured and only three survived. Most were officially listed as from FANY in a nod to the Geneva Convention that women in the services were not to bear arms – not always very practical in the SOE during combat. Of the twelve murdered by the Nazis, one was the Jewish agent Denise Bloch. A thirteenth woman was the Jewish agent Muriel Byck, who died from exhaustion and meningitis in May 1944 after six weeks of intense work in the field.

Denise Madeleine Bloch, codename Ambroise, came officially from FANY and was awarded the King's Commendation for Brave Conduct, Legion d'Honneur, *Croix de Guerre avec Palme* and *Medaille de la Résistance avec Rosette*. She was murdered by the Nazis at Ravensbrück along with Violette Szabo and Lilian Rolfe between 25 January and 2 February 1945. Following terrible treatment, the three women were eventually shot in the back of the neck after SS officers had ordered them to kneel.

SOE's chief cryptographer throughout most of the war was Leo Marks; he had briefed Denise Bloch and given her a 'code-poem' which he had composed himself. This was to decipher messages and originally used well-known poems. The Germans soon worked this out, so Marks began to compose his own. The one he wrote for Violette Szabo, 'The Life that I Have', became well-known after the war.

The life that I have
Is all that I have
And the life that I have
Is yours.

The love that I have
Of the life that I have
Is yours and yours and yours.

A sleep I shall have
A rest I shall have
Yet death will be but a pause.

For the peace of my years
In the long green grass
Will be yours and yours and yours.

The poem was used in the 1958 film about Szabo, *Carve Her Name with Pride*. Marks jokingly described himself as the 'Poet Laureate of Signals'.

Marks was considered too much of a misfit to work at Bletchley Park and so was sent to SOE where he was credited with developing, if not inventing, the one-time letter pad. SOE was described as 'a mixture of brilliant brains and bungling amateurs'. That certainly was the view of Marks, expressed clearly in his book *Between Silk and Cyanide* that was not published until 1998 because government censors had sat on it for nearly 20 years. Marks was not at all polite about the SOE leadership especially after the *Das Englandspiel* debacle in the Netherlands. German counter-intelligence did not automatically shoot SOE radio operators out of hand, even though they had a life expectancy of about six weeks. The Germans would try to turn them instead. Marks had worked out that perhaps the whole Netherland network was compromised in what the Germans were calling the 'English game'. Marks's warnings were ignored in SOE and perhaps as many as 50 further agents were sent to their deaths.

Marks's memoir is one of the wittiest accounts of spying and code-breaking during the Second World War. For example, he described one of his superiors as 'a problem to which no solution compatible with law was in sight'; 'a one-man obstacle course, the colonel was opposed to any kind of change except in his rank'.

Leopold Samuel Marks, MBE, became famous after the war not least as a screenwriter. He wrote the script for the very controversial *Peeping Tom* (1960) an early slasher film that was lambasted at the time but decades later was often considered a masterpiece.

What the Resistance achieved

The Jewish resistance achieved a great deal in terms of self-respect, but what did the overall resistance movement achieve in the Second World War? Opinions, as ever, vary among historians. Field Marshal Albert Kesselring, who commanded German forces in Italy, admitted that eliminating the partisans had been of 'capital importance'. Churchill had noted that the Italian partisans had effectively tied down six of the twenty-five German divisions. Halik Kochanski's recent magisterial work on the underground war in Europe concludes that it was useful but not crucial, except in the provision of intelligence. She argues that the SOE's role in creating networks has been exaggerated. The image or memory of the resistance was more important to the concept of the nation state, especially in France, she concluded.

Chapter Eight

Revenge

The Jewish Brigade soldiers were about to leave their Italian base in Tarvisio and were told they were moving into Germany. After parade, the legendary Sergeant Israel Carmi walked to the white chalk square in front of the flagpole. The soldiers would listen carefully, because he carried the weight of authority of the Haganah as well as his Special Night Squad reputation and his distinguished combat record in the Brigade.

He made it clear that a Jewish army wearing the Star of David on the shoulder as a sign of pride, not submission, would soon be entering Deutschland as an occupying force. Speechifying did not come easily to Carmi, so he read from a speech prepared by Haganah officers more senior than himself. Despite the slightly stilted rendition, the great passion in his voice moved his audience. Inter alia, he said:

1. Hate the butchers of your people – unto all generations.
2. Remember: the Jewish Brigade in Nazi Germany is a Jewish army of occupation.
3. Remember: the fact that we come as a military unit with flag and emblem in sight of the German people, in its homeland – vengeance.
4. Remember: vengeance is a communal task. Any irresponsible act weakens the group.
5. Look like a Jew who is proud of his people and his flag
6. Your duty: dedication, loyalty and love for the remnants of the sword and the camps.

Carmi said little more, although he had already declared almost the new ten commandments of retribution for the sons of Yahweh. He folded his notes away and put them back into his shirt pocket.

He was about to return to the ranks but he called out to his fellow fighters in a strong passionate voice: 'Cursed be he who fails to remember what they have done to us!'

The troops shouted out 'Amen' from a thousand and more voices.

The parade was dismissed. In the morning the Jewish Brigade would drive north, conquerors marching into the remains of the Thousand-Year Reich, just a few weeks after the death of the Nazi leader who had made that boast of a thousand years. It had been long agreed with the British War Office that their olive green trucks would boast a Star of David painted in bright yellow on the bumpers. A large blue-and-white 'national' flag hung from the back of the truck cabs. Unauthorised messages had been chalked in German on the sides of the vehicles: '*Die Juden kommen.*' And also: '*Kein Reich, kein Volk, kein Führer.*'[1]

Carmi had vengeance in his heart but he had already practised the discipline he urged on his men. On a number of occasions, he had prevented both surrendering Wehrmacht and SS being killed. He told those threatening them: 'If you want to kill Germans, kill them in combat.' Revenge was best tasted cold but also in a disciplined manner.

The German wasteland

What did total German defeat mean? At least a decade of poverty, hunger, fear, ruins, violence, black markets, foreign occupation and Teutonic hard work. The Nazis deployed millions of slave labourers and now the Germans had to do all the hard work themselves. Former Nazi members were organised in work gangs to clear the rubble. 'Those summoned to comply must provide their own suitable tools.' This summons was accompanied in some cases by the threat that if 'you fail to appear, freed political prisoners will make sure that you do'. It was not until 1977 that the last rubble clearance brigade, in Dresden, was able to lay down its tools.[2]

And always the silence, the silence about the murdered millions shimmered like a ghost in the background. Everyone claimed not to know – but they were nearly always lying.

Everyone talked of Zero Hour, a fresh start but in the head offices, courts and universities of the occupation zones and, later, the Federal Republic, the Nazi elite cheerfully carried on. The de-Nazification programmes achieved very little, especially when the Allies needed not only the same administrators to run the destroyed Western half of the former Reich but also recruited thousands of spies to help them counter the new rulers of the eastern half of Europe, especially in the new organisation of General Reinhard Gehlen. He had been the head of military intelligence on the Eastern Front and remained the West German spy chief for two decades, employing many of his former Gestapo and SS subordinates. Meanwhile, the Americans were courting with big loud salaries and quiet amnesties, numerous scientists, especially the ones associated with the wonder weapons. Dr Wernher van Braun was just the best known of many.

In the summer of 1945 about 75 million people lived in the four occupation zones of Germany. Around 40 million, more than half, were not where they belonged or wanted to be because the Nazi war had acted as a powerful abduction machine. Millions were former prisoners of the Germans or slave workers but also millions of German soldiers had surrendered, especially in the West. Ordinary German citizens were terrified of the roving wolf packs, as they often saw them, of former slave workers from the east.

Surviving near-naked Jews in the camps were sometimes forced to wear the discarded uniforms of their SS guards. Over a hundred thousand Jews flowed into Germany from the east. Of all places, Munich, the birthplace of the Nazi movement, became a hub. Most Jews wanted to go to America or Palestine and so American-occupied Bavaria was, they hoped, a halfway house to their promised lands. Continuing pogroms in Russian-controlled Poland drove even more Jews westwards. For example, in Kielce, ninety miles south of Warsaw, terrible atrocities were inflicted on Jews a year after the end of the war.

Millions of Germans deported from the east were quicker to adapt to the new circumstances and became a blessing to the German economy. These displaced persons had lost all their illusions, and property, and were more flexible in their attitudes to how they could earn an income. The incoming German displaced persons were hated by the local residents, so much so that both the Americans and British feared that a civil war could break out between them.

The roads were full of people crossing the continent on foot, sometimes dragging carts, because public transport was almost non-existent. In the summer of 1947, the *Neue Illustrierte* newspaper commissioned its photographer to take a night train from Hamburg to Munich. It took him eight days. The trains that did run were packed but many were either cancelled or had to stop in the middle of the countryside because the tracks had been destroyed by bombing.

While many Germans barricaded themselves in, others basked in the new friendships; evacuation and mass migration aroused curiosity as well as fear. The experience of actually or potentially losing everything and the reduction of hierarchies and the differences between rich and poor led to many new relationships as well as a classless dance-hall fad. The 'freedom of the dispossessed' took hold amid the squalor and misery.

The occupying Allies were not supposed to fraternise but with so many single women, young widows, or married *Frauen* disillusioned with the returning army of burnt-out men, it was difficult not to engage, especially as the Americans were blessed with so much chocolate and chewing gum and so many good-quality cigarettes. The German photographer and actress Hildegard Knef put it baldly: 'The German men lost the war, now they want to win it again in the bedroom.'

So many German men had been killed and millions were languishing in Allied PoW camps and millions were starving in Russian camps. It was said that 1945 Germany was a land of women. Some were very independent as they had to navigate far and wide, where no phones worked, to forage for food in the black market. Others were cowed by the naked male aggression of the Red Army's rape frenzies. In addition, millions of freed forced labourers, often with severe mental disorders, roamed the streets. And, although it was hushed up, many German women were raped by Allied soldiers as well. Despite all the dangers, men and women seemed often to exude an exuberance that, somehow, they had survived. Besides dance halls, the cinemas still standing or makeshift halls were full as well. Many of the new productions were dubbed 'rubble films' of life and love amid the destruction. Wolfgang Liebeneiner, a well-known actor and director, in 1950 made a film called *Abundance of Life* (*Des Lebens Überfluss*) about the new freedoms of young people. It was called the last of the 'rubble films'.[3]

For many Allied troops, occupied Germany was like the Wild West, especially if they had a taste for black-market free enterprise. For the Jewish soldiers returning it was usually hell on earth as nearly all of them failed to find the families they left behind.

Running the ruined Reich

It had been agreed at the Yalta conference in February 1945 that Austria and Germany would be administered by the US, UK and the USSR with a smaller zone for France. An Allied Control Commission was set up in Berlin, although co-operation with USSR soon largely broke down. Without the German-speaking refugees from the 'King's Most Loyal Aliens' in the Pioneer Corps and then the specialist combat and intelligence services, the British could not have administered their zone of occupation. Similarly, the Americans relied on their graduates from Camp Ritchie. Thousands of Jewish servicemen and women were assigned to the British Control Commission and BAOR (British Army of the Rhine). Many were sent back to their former German and Austrian towns where they could go to their surviving town halls and police stations to look up the usually immaculate Germans records of which police and Nazi officials had persecuted alleged opponents of the regime, especially Jews. Much of the work was administration and translation but tens of thousands of German PoWs had to be interrogated, not least to hunt for Nazi war criminals and gathering evidence for the War Crimes Investigation Unit.

All the laws had to be democratised and redrafted (and passed by the four occupying powers) so German-speaking former lawyers serving in the Allied forces were in great demand. The jobs of others were even more specialised and high profile. For example, John Langford (Erwin

Lehmann, born in East Prussia) transferred from the Pioneer Corps to the 6th Airborne Division and then returned to Germany to guard Winston Churchill and Clement Attlee, the Labour leader, at the Potsdam Conference in July 1945. Another German refugee, Edward Norton, who was born in Mannheim, also protected the British leaders.[4] The so-called Big Three changed during the conference – in the middle of it Clement Attlee took over as British Prime Minister which neither Joseph Stalin nor President Harry S. Truman could understand after Churchill's victory in the war just ended. In another paradox, Truman informed the Russian leader that the USA was about to launch a new kind of weapon against the Japanese. Stalin's spies, especially the Anglo-German Klaus Fuchs, had informed him long before Truman had even heard of the successful atomic bomb project. And another strange thing: Britain had gone to war ostensibly because of Poland, but the Soviet-backed Polish communist group was to take over the country.

One of the main purposes of Potsdam was to avoid another Treaty of Versailles that allegedly sowed the seeds for the Second World War in Europe. And yet Germany's border was moved westward to the Oder-Neisse line and the Russians stripped their zone of nearly everything that could be moved to Russia, including whole factories. The Reich had surrendered unconditionally, so the victors could do what they wanted. As the anti-German hot war slid into the anti-Soviet Cold War, the Western mantra became how to keep the Germans down, the Russians out and Americans in. This is what the North Atlantic Treaty Organization achieved four years later.

Not all the interrogators served in Germany or Austria. Britain had numerous German PoW camps at home, with the prisoners graded according to whether they were pro- or anti-Nazi. They were graded black, grey or white, with the camps for the black PoWs being farthest north.

In October 1945 Viennese-born Eric Saunders (Ignaz Schwartz) returned from SOE duties in Italy and became an interpreter at Norton Fitzwarren, just outside Taunton. Some of the interrogators were also 'volunteered' to teach 'democracy courses' to their charges.

Many of the Ritchie Boys and the British German-speakers became involved with setting up new media in their occupied zones. Hamburg was in the British zone and Radio Hamburg became the military government station. They had to broadcast news and new regulations, curfew hours and details of food rationing for example. Bread was rationed in Britain for the first time in order to feed starving Germans. The German-speakers in British uniform also tried to start re-education about the Nazi past as well as broadcast lists of missing persons to help re-unite families. In May 1945 Geoffrey Perry (Horst Pinschewer) read the first news from the same microphone that two days earlier William Joyce (Lord Haw-Haw) used to give his farewell message to the Germans. And then the notorious Fascist went into hiding. By amazing chance Geoffrey Perry, who was out collecting firewood for his stove, bumped into the same William Joyce in a forest near to the broadcast station and engaged him in conversation. The polite German told the British soldiers where they could easily find wood and the German seemed to know a lot about trees. The British Jewish serviceman then asked whether he was the notorious broadcaster and he said 'no', that he was a German. As he put his hands in his pocket, either to get his papers or his gun, the Jewish soldier aimed at his hand but shot him accidentally in the backside. As Perry tried to patch up the four holes in the victim's rear, a soldier accompanying Perry looked through the pockets and found a German ID and, luckily, a second Abwehr intelligence ID with Joyce's name was also found. It would have been very embarrassing for a British serviceman to shoot an unarmed German civilian. That a German in British uniform should have the honour of capturing this famous traitor was not without irony.[5]

Jewish servicemen were also involved with the grisly task of liberating concentration camps. On 14 April 1945 British troops liberated Bergen-Belsen. Two Jewish army chaplains began administering to the spiritual needs of the desperately ill survivors while medics provided physical support. The psychological horrors never left many of those who first witnessed the death camps.

War Crimes

Many Jewish servicemen and women worked extensively on hunting down and then prosecuting Nazi war criminals. The British Nazi hunters tried to capture their prey alive and bring them to trial. Captain Howard Alexander (Hans Alexander), originally from the Pioneer Corps, returned to his homeland and one of his first tasks was to interrogate Irma Grese, the infamous 'Beast of Belsen'. He gave up as she was a totally hardened and unrepentant prisoner, who was eventually hanged. Captain Alexander then joined a team hunting for Rudolf Hoess, the commandant of Auschwitz. He was traced to a small farmhouse near Flensburg by shadowing his wife; Hoess was eventually caught in early March 1946. He had gone to extremes to change his identity and looks but he kept wearing his wedding ring with the date of his marriage.

The British War Crimes Investigation Unit was based at BAOR HQ in Bad Oeynhausen, near Lübeck. The unit concentrated on members of the SS and senior Nazi officials, as well as senior army, naval and intelligence personnel. The unit also investigated the *Kapos* – the Jewish guards who formed part of the camp administration. The *Kapos* were often more brutal than the SS. As war crimes trials were held throughout the country, every town and city needed the Jewish refugees in uniform to act as translators in the courts.

The main trials were held at Nuremberg, where the Nazis had held their most iconoclastic rallies. Much of the legal infrastructure was provided by the Americans, although all four victors had extensive legal teams. Originally, the British government was in favour of summary executions for the senior Nazis; the Americans, however, insisted on tribunals. Senior Jewish lawyers such as the Viennese-born Stephen Stewart (Stephen Strauss) played a key role in the prosecuting teams. He was also the chief prosecutor at a separate trial to prosecute those responsible for the torture and deaths of hundreds of thousands of women in the Ravensbrück concentration camp. At the start of this Stewart addressed the question that the trials were merely victors' justice. He insisted that this was not true in fact or law, although history has continued to debate this. If Hitler had not turned on his Jewish scientists, he may just have got the A-bomb before his enemies. Churchill might then have been in the dock as a war criminal.

Unofficial Nazi-hunting operations

Some key members of the Jewish Brigade went off in various missions to rescue Jews and punish Nazis. This was particularly so of the Brigade when it was based in Tarvisio, near the border triangle of Italy, Yugoslavia and Austria. Inevitably, Israel Carmi was heavily involved in the hunt for Nazis as well as providing emergency aid to Jewish survivors, especially children, and then their passage to Palestine. The work of the Brigade, in uniform and using British Army vehicles, meant co-operating with the *Bricha* (it means flight or escape) movement that aided *Aliyah* (emigration) to Palestine. They even bought or stole boats to get the displaced persons (DPs) to the promised land.

The core execution group of the Brigade was partly led by Israel Carmi. He assembled his main volunteers in a farmhouse sequestered near their Tarvisio base and said: 'This is family business. Only Jews can do what has to be done.' He did not ask for or take questions after his briefing. One soldier said later there could be secret courts to create some notion of justice. Carmi replied: 'I will be the judge *and* jury.'[6]

The Brigade worked with Jewish groups who had survived and who formed assassination squads known as *Nakam* (revenge). The Brigade members referred to this unofficial work as TTG (*Tilhas Tizig Gesheften* – literally 'kiss my arse business'. The exact figure is unknown but the TTG business may have summarily executed 1,500 Nazis.

Meir Zorea had earned an MC as a lieutenant in the Brigade and later became a member of the Knesset and a general in the Israel Defence Forces. He had been a member of a revenge squad and he recalled:

We only eliminated those directly involved in the slaughter of Jews. At first we put a bullet through their heads. Then we strangled them. With our bare hands. We never said anything before we killed them. Not why or who we were. We just killed them like you kill a bug.

The Brigade avengers went to a number of just liberated camps and on one occasion a group of living skeletons, obviously near death, managed to summon their last bits of energy to ask about the Star of David on the vehicle bumpers and on the shoulder flashes.

'We are a Jewish army,' one Brigade member said.

A very old man said he was a rabbi and came up and asked to touch the Brigade soldier's hands. 'I want to see if you are real,' he said in Yiddish. 'I can't believe there is a Jewish army. You must be angels.'

The Brigade soldier embraced the dying survivor.

In July 1945 the Brigade left for Belgium and the Netherlands; it was disbanded in the following year. Many of its key officers and NCOs had already left the Brigade and important players such as Israel Carmi were sent back to Europe by the Yishuv to re-organise the *Bricha* and especially the migration to Palestine. Occasionally, the assembly points for the *Aliyah* were former concentration camps (for example, Judenberg a sub-camp of Mauthausen). In the city of Graz, a well-known *Bricha* figure, nicknamed Pini the Red (Pinchas Zeitag), was responsible for transport in Italy. Much of the transport was supplied by the Brigade while they were based in Northern Italy. British military lorries and jeeps would take the DPs to the Brigade's motor depot at Pontebba. They were given fresh food, shower facilities and new clothing as well as medical examinations and a comfortable place to sleep. Within a few days they were transported to *hachsharot* in Bari, Bologna or Modena; this was a training centre for preparation (*hachshara* training: Hebrew: הַכְשָׁרָה) for agricultural work in the kibbutzim in Palestine. The Brigade and *Bricha* perhaps moved about 20,000 DPs to Palestine. Much of the costs for the successful exodus were arranged by American Jewish organisations although the British War Office supplied much of the logistics, unwittingly. In a broader operation known as ALIYAH BET, around 250,000 DPs were rapidly shipped to Palestine after the revival of Polish pogroms in 1946.

Nakam

Individual Jews in Germany also sought revenge on their Nazi persecutors. The Nuremberg trials ended in the convictions of just 161 senior individuals (although there were other trials around Germany and in Austria and France). Originally the Allies had estimated that there were millions who should be put on trial and who were still living in West Germany. By the end of the 1940s, however, only a hundred Nazis remained in prison.

A group of about fifty young men and women who had survived the ghettoes and the partisan groups in the forests set up a revenge movement. It was also called *Nakam* and it was led by Abba Kovner who grew up in what is now Vilnius, Lithuania. Forced into the ghetto when the Germans occupied the area, in early 1942 he published a manifesto called 'Let us not go like lambs to the slaughter'. Although the authorship of this radical manifesto has been debated, it made clear that Hitler wanted to destroy all Jews, and that the work camps were a euphemism for slaughter. So Kovner insisted that the Jews should die fighting: Kovner and others formed the first armed groups in the ghettos. Kovner's group and others were known as the Avengers (*Nokmim*). His Vilnius group fought as partisans with other local fighters, some Soviet-led, until the Red Army liberated Vilnius in July 1944. Then Kovner became one of the leaders of the *Bricha* movement.

Nakam was also called *Dam Yisrael Noter* ('the blood of Israel avenges'; the acronym DIN also means 'judgement'). Two big plans were hatched; one was to kill millions of Germans by poisoning the water supplies: Hamburg, Frankfurt, Munich and Nuremberg were, inter alia, selected and the estimate of fatalities was, yes, six million. The plotters did a lot of research on water systems and a suitable poison. The Yishuv leaders were informed but their support was very tepid because they feared that the moral case for Israel's independence would be harmed by mass murder, especially if any Allied personnel were also harmed. Some scientists were recruited but were told only that the poison was to kill SS prisoners.

Kovner selected a small, balding man from Lithuania, Joseph Harmatz, as his chief of 'special operations'. Unofficial death sentences were imposed on senior Nazis still at large. Some were found dead in roadside ditches, apparently cut down by hit-and-run drivers, others met their end in accidents involving mysterious technical failures of their vehicles. One senior Gestapo officer was waiting for a minor operation in hospital when, somehow, kerosene got into his bloodstream. In all, dozens of senior Nazis were killed by the *Nakam* vigilantes.

But the avengers were still keen on a big spectacular as they became increasingly frustrated by the lack of progress of the war crimes tribunals.

In April 1946 Harmatz was the main organiser of the plot aimed at Stalag 13, a detention centre for former SS men near Nuremberg. The prisoners were supplied by a single bakery where a *Nakam* man had secured a job as a trainee baker. The poison plan was to take place on a Saturday night because the black bread delivered on the Sunday would be eaten only by the Germans. The American guards had white bread on Sunday. Using an artist's brush, Harmatz painted 3,000 loaves of black bread with a mixture of arsenic and glue. 'Each prisoner got a quarter of a loaf and that meant 12,000,' Harmatz confessed in his 1998 memoir *From the Wings*. Some of the Germans were suspicious but 1,900 men suffered acute food poisoning. Harmatz later claimed that he had killed hundreds of SS soldiers but others including American sources say there were no fatalities. The remaining plans were aborted when the British arrested Kovner; it was rumoured he was set up by the Yishuv. Kovner then fled to join the Haganah in December 1947, where he fought as a captain in the war of independence. He later became one of the greatest authors of modern Hebrew poetry. Harmatz also later fled to Israel where he ran a shipping line. In 2000, following an appearance on a TV programme about the bakery plot, Nuremberg police announced that they were investigating Harmatz and other Avengers. Trying to prosecute Holocaust survivors for trying to kill Nazis prompted the Nuremberg authorities not to proceed 'because of extraordinary circumstances'. The trial might have also thrown up some of the seedier sides of *Nakam*: Harmatz had, for example, been a *Kapo* in the Vilnius ghetto and was also for a while an NKVD operative.

Two very British forms of action

The 43 Group

This was a British anti-fascist organisation set up by some distinguished Jewish ex-servicemen to resist anti-Semitic groups in the UK such as the Union Movement, the new party founded by Sir Oswald Mosley, the pro-Nazi leader, on his release from prison. In April 1946, forty-three people came together in a room of Maccabi House, a Jewish sports centre in Hampstead, London. The group included Gerald Flamberg, a middleweight boxing champion who served with the Parachute Regiment at Arnhem, where he earned the Military Medal. Leonard Sherman was a martial arts expert and former Welsh Guardsman. These were useful men to have in any street brawls or to stop violent attacks on London Jews and Jewish property. The numbers of Jews working to stop fascist attacks and anti-Semitic rallies grew to over 300 people including the VC holder, Tommy Gould.

The 43 Group published an anti-racist paper called *On Guard* to report on Mosley supporters especially. The Board of Deputies of British Jews was rather wary of the 43 Group as it sought to prevent the Union Movement mobilising support on the streets in the way that had happened in Germany and in Britain before 1939. The official Jewish organisations were worried about any Jewish activism, particularly at a time when militant Zionist groups such as the Irgun were attacking Mandate authorities in Palestine. The 43 Group disbanded itself voluntarily in June 1950 as it considered the fascist resurgence danger had passed.

SAS Nazi Hunters

The aftermath of Operation LOYTON was, and to an extent still is, one of the most secret ops of the Second World War. Between 12 August and 9 October 1944, eighty SAS men parachuted into the Vosges mountains in north-eastern France. They were tasked with creating mayhem hundreds of miles behind enemy lines. Unfortunately, the German forces were reinforcing the area against General George Patton's Third Army. A week or so became two months. With their supplies and ammunition running low, the SAS were ordered to form small break-out groups to reach Allied lines. During the intensive manhunt by powerful German forces, including crack SS troops, thirty-one men were captured and later executed by the Germans. Also, all the male residents aged between 16 and 60 of Moussey, a village near the first SAS camp, were deported to Germany. After the war only seventy of the 210 men deported returned from the camps.

Some of the elite troops who survived the operation vowed to hunt the killers who had tortured and executed British PoWs. But the SAS was about to be disbanded at the end of the war. Many top brass had always disliked the swashbuckling rogues who seemed to them to inhabit the SAS. More traditional warriors disliked the scarce resources given to the special forces and the way they hoovered up many of the best NCOs and officers from the regular forces.

Lieutenant Colonel Brian Franks had been in command of part of the operation on the ground in France. He was determined to organise, fund and lead an unofficial SAS mission to get the killers of thirty-one of his colleagues. Winston Churchill backed him to the hilt but he was no longer prime minster. Churchill had always called for post-war retribution but the Foreign Office avoided all mention of post-war witch-hunts on foreign soil. So, it was all done *sotto voce*. The mission was to continue from the last months of the war until 1948.[7]

The leader of the hunters was Major Eric 'Bill' Barkworth, a 'man of iron principle, unbreakable spirit and a maverick singlemindedness almost without compare'.[8] And yet he got to see Hitler's secret 'Commando Order' only in January 1945. It was clear to him that some of the SAS men had been killed but he would find out what happened to them and render justice. SAS Colonel Brian Franks knew that a great deal of retributive justice would be enforced against the big fish, but Franks and Barkworth would continue to chase the 'small' war criminals who had murdered their colleagues. It was a smaller war but a very personal and intense one.

One of the men on the lists of wanted by the secret SAS team was *Standartenführer* Dr Erich Isselhorst who gave himself up to the US Seventh Army. He not only ingratiated himself with the Americans but he understood that they were looking for counter-intelligence experts; he had worked in that field on the Eastern front and US military intelligence officers were building up their assets to combat the USSR.

Meanwhile Barkworth had set up a base and cellar prison in the Villa Degler, an isolated large house in Gaggenau on the edge of the Black Forest just over the border from France. The cellars were used as a small prison. And he had one suspect there already: *Hauptsturmführer* Karl Buck who was singing like a canary, helped by Barkworth's almost perfect German and not any violence. An interrogator without equal, his prisoners were offered a chance to confess and supply evidence against their superiors or they could expect no clemency at the forthcoming war crimes tribunals. Every German interrogated by Barkworth always commented on his courtesy and consideration. So, Buck in the end passed the buck: he had ordered the Rotenfels prison commandant to shoot the British and American prisoners, thus carrying out Isselhorst's orders. The old excuse of just obeying orders.

The SAS team was usually only about a maximum of twelve men with a single officer in charge, with just four war-worn jeeps. The American War Crimes Investigation team members working on the same cases in Gaggenau were amazed. They had two pathologists, several professional interrogators, two legal experts plus shorthand typists and photographers and good kit. On one occasion the SAS hunters had resorted to a Ouija board and it led amazingly to the discovery of two Canadian airmen's bodies. When this was discovered in Whitehall the mandarins went ballistic and one SAS officer was threatened with being charged with 'conduct unbecoming an officer and a gentleman'.

German-speaking Jews were plentiful in the SAS before disbandment. Some had come over from remnants of the Special Interrogation Group and the X Troop. One of the original eighty SAS men who went in first on Operation LOYTON was Sergeant Robert Lodge, in fact Rudolf Friedlander, a German Jew who had settled in West London and had already earned the Distinguished Conduct Medal. At 33 he was one of the oldest SAS troopers but in spite of this and thick jam-jar glasses he had a fine fighting reputation in the regiment. Although Barkworh spoke almost prefect German, it was logical that he tapped into the battle-hardened German-speaking Jewish volunteers to augment his highly secret group of hunters. One of these was Captain Harry Stevens (Hans Schweiger, an Austrian who had served in 12 Force SOE) who worked as part of the Official War Crimes Unit.

In searching for some of the SAS bodies – all hope of finding any alive had gone – the worst place was under the prison in nearby Strasbourg. SAS Sergeant Sandy Rhodes had to go into a large room where a lot of experiments on human bodies had been carried out.

> It was absolutely full of human body parts, all preserved in formalin in tanks … . There were heads and faces and arms and legs; if one saw possibly a tattoo on an arm which one knew from regimental badges or English sayings … . There was a possibility that some of our people could have been there.[9]

Luckily Rhodes found no evidence of any chopped-up SAS troopers although his colleagues had suffered dreadful torture.

Churchill continued secretly to back the mission. Throughout the war he had challenged the military to find 'hunter troops for a butcher-and-bolt reign of terror'. The prime minister knew that many of the missions would end in death and he backed to the hilt those warriors who heeded his call.

The MP for West Dorset, Simon Wingfield Digby, asked a question in the House of Commons about special forces fighting in southern Europe.

> Is it true, Prime Minister, that there is a body of our men out in the Aegean islands, fighting under the Union flag, that are nothing short of being a band of murderous, renegade cut-throats?

Churchill shot back with a famous riposte: 'If you do not take your seat and keep quiet, I will send you out to join them.' The MP stayed in the seat for another thirty years but Churchill was soon out of power. Without Churchill's secret protection and that of his son Randolph, who had served with the SAS, the top brass would have closed down the SAS for ever. They hated its maverick style and disliked intensely so many foreigners serving in the regiment and even, God forbid, the occasional civilian. Colonel Franks enjoyed the Leader of the Opposition's total support. Churchill had been wary when he advocated special forces – much of it was based in the Ministry of Economic Warfare especially the SOE, where many of Churchill's raiders came from. With both Churchills backing them, the SAS Nazi hunters played the long game in Whitehall.

The 2nd SAS HQ in Glebe House in Colchester was about to close and so the Nazi Hunters in France would lose their communications base in the UK. Another HQ was set up in 20 Eaton Square while the Barkworth unit would 'go dark' and yet hide in plain sight. BAOR had been hostile but the secret SAS unit would operate under a general war crimes cover. They were now known in a small intelligence circle as the 'Secret Hunters'. Officially, however, they were known as SAS WCIT – War Crimes Investigation Team.

With Churchill's fall from power the SOE was about to be chopped as well. Vera Atkins, who was a leading light in SOE's French Section, was born into a Jewish family with a Romanian father and an English mother. Settling in England in the early 1930s with her mother after her father's death, Atkins came to the attention of MI6 and was heavily involved in intelligence work by the time war was declared in September 1939. Once the war in Europe ended in May 1945, she had a burning desire to discover what had happened to the forty or so French Section agents who had been captured by the Nazis, especially the fifteen women agents who had seemingly disappeared without trace, including Noor Inayat Khan, Violette Szabo, Lilian Rolfe and Denise Bloch, who was Jewish. The last three women were murdered at the same time at Ravensbrück concentration camp in February 1945 along with another female agent, Cicely Lefort. With the help of SAS investigators looking into cases of men from the regiment who had been taken prisoner by the Germans and executed, she found out that four SOE female agents had been given lethal injections by SS executioners at Natzweiler concentration camp in

Alsace and thrust into the ovens in the camp's crematorium whilst still breathing; one severely tortured woman had managed to rake the face of one her torturers as she was pushed in and burnt. The red weals had aided his discovery. Atkins then joined the SAS at Degler House.

Vera Atkins, whose family name was Rosenberg, was welcomed by the SAS hunters. True, she was a woman and Jewish as well but she had been the dominant force in the French SOE section, the brains behind the nominal boss, Maurice Buckmaster, its rather ineffectual head. She was a very resolute multi-lingual hunter herself. She, too, had many secrets to hide, not least that she was officially an enemy alien, despite the incredible effort she put into her over-accentuated cut-glass English accent. Because of her Romanian background, the security file on her never seemed to decide whether she was suspected of being a German or a Russian agent. She was passed over for a gong for nearly fifty years because of lingering Foreign Office suspicions. Yet she was the right person at the right time, especially for those seeking revenge for war crimes. She said:

> I went to find them as a private enterprise. I wanted to know. I always thought 'missing presumed dead' to be such a terrible verdict.[10]

She continued for the rest of her life to defend the SOE's role in sending so many female agents to France. She not only protected her organisation but she also advised on the many books and films on the subject. Perhaps the best-known was the 1958 movie on Violette Szabo, *Carve Her Name with Pride*, starring Virginia McKenna and Paul Scofield.

On 5 October 1945, 1st and 2nd SAS held their disbandment parades and the men prepared to return to their 'home' regiments, or volunteer for other airborne units or go back to 'civvy street'. That left Barkworth's unit the only surviving SAS operation. Despite now operating clandestinely, the Secret Hunters still wore the distinctive SAS beret and would proudly display their winged dagger insignia bearing their timeless motto 'Who Dares Wins'. In the post-war confusion at the War Office the team also still got paid.

BAOR did everything to shut down the Secret Hunters who had now grown to four officers and twenty-one men. Nevertheless, despite the extra personnel, the constant work and BAOR pressure eventually ground down Barkworth who seemed to need hardly any sleep. Yet his sense of humour had not left him, not least after being hospitalised following an unfortunate incident with a German dentist who had extracted a tooth. The major's face had swollen badly. 'He must have been a Werewolf,' he quipped. The Werewolves were supposed to be Hitler's last throw with a national underground army to destroy the invaders. The Werewolves were an occasional irritant, not a national rebellion.

Barkworth asked his colourful fixer in London, Captain Prince Yurka Galitzine, a fabulously effective black operator and a white Russian who had served with the SAS, to help him gain access to some of his quarries who were hiding in the Russian and US zones. Both administrations were often unhelpful to the Brits.

In May 1946 the first SAS war crimes tribunals opened, at the Zoological Gardens in Wuppertal, just north of Cologne in the British Zone. It was made clear from the start that acting under orders was no excuse, not least because they went to extraordinary lengths to hide their crimes – stripping the victims, burning their clothing and burying their ID tags, for example. All but one of eleven captured and held by the SAS were found guilty: five were given prison sentences of up to ten years and five received death sentences. Others were to be passed over to French authorities for crimes committed in France. Some received only two or three years in prison. The punishments did not seem to fit the crime, in some cases.

Other trials followed, especially of crimes against the SOE women. Peter Straub, Natzweiler camp executioner, got only thirteen years for putting the SOE agents, one still living, in the crematorium. The Hunters felt that, after all their efforts, the courts had been too lenient. On 2 June Captain Galitzine was so angry that the Natzweiler case – the camp was considered the Belsen of France – resulted in such lenient judgements, against all the rules, the white Russian prince, a former journalist and once a now repentant member of a pre-war anti-Semitic group wrote an article anonymously for the *Sunday Express*. The headline shouted out: 'FOUR BRITISH GIRLS BURNED ALIVE – ONE GERMAN TO DIE. GIRL FOUGHT AT OVEN DOOR.'

The Secret Hunters felt that their men had been grossly tortured and killed while the courts were handing out lenient sentences. They hoped that the media furore caused by the *Sunday Express* story could possibly increase the severity of the sentences handed down in the next round of trials.

Although some of the more senior SS and Gestapo men justified the murder of the SAS men according to Hitler's Commando Order, it did not wash. The senior men were sentenced to death by hanging, including Barkworth's main target Erich Isselhorst, a lawyer and mass murderer. He was handed over to the French and 'officially executed' but the wily Isselhorst may have been absorbed into the Gehlen Organisation.

The Secret Hunters eventually emerged from the dark because they had achieved so much with so little. Barkworth's team had gained so much expertise that London began to task them with a range of missions, mainly regarding SAS and SBS troops, including the Cockleshell Heroes, Operation FRANKTON. In mid-1948 the British government announced an end to all the war crimes tribunals, right in the middle of the Stalag Luft trials regarding the murders of seventy escapees from the Stalag Luft PoW camp, otherwise known as the Great Escape using three tunnels, Tom, Dick and Harry. Because of the public uproar, the second Stalag Luft trial was completed. The SAS trials were done but many more were not; the details were put in secret files for many decades. What mattered now was rehabilitating the creation of the Federal Republic of Germany out of the three occupation zones run by the Western Allies in the Cold War with the USSR.

Barkworth had employed a young German secretary from nearby Karlsruhe to work in the unofficial SAS HQ at Degler House. In one happy ending, they fell in love and were married.

One or two of the SAS main suspects had escaped but the Regiment had survived and got justice for some of their men who had been murdered by the Nazis. In July 1947, to simplify a complicated story, the Artists' Rifles regiment – a volunteer light infantry unit – merged with the 'officially' disbanded SAS to form 21st Special Air Service Regiment (Artists). This was a Territorial Army unit but it did mean the partial resurrection of the SAS and, fittingly, Brian Franks was the first commanding officer.[11] In the run up to the Korean War the SAS was fully re-established as a regular unit. Barkworth and his team had hunted down over 100 Germans guilty of atrocities despite the tiny resources and the often Jobsworth attitudes in the BAOR and the War Office. The SAS had again dared and – largely – won. And the SAS was back in action around the world.

Chapter Nine

Legacy

Churchill was correct. His idea to set up or allow German-speaking special forces was a good one. The Special Interrogation Group achieved a lot although Buck's plans were often thwarted. The SIG men were what Martin Sugarman called true 'Lions of Judah' in their incredible bravery. On a bigger canvas the X Troop was extremely successful especially in the Normandy landings.

Those were the advantages for British war aims.

The Jewish fighters also inspired self-respect among the hundreds of thousands of Jews who had survived the Holocaust. This was particularly true of the Jewish Brigade – Holocaust survivors who met them in the camps sometimes assumed they were angels, so amazing was the concept of a Jewish army.

Jews had reluctantly celebrated their underdog victories from David and Goliath, the Israelites who escaped from the pharaoh, to the Maccabee brothers who defeated the Greek Empire. The fight back had begun really with Orde Wingate's vision and the Haganah's military plans to preserve the Yishuv. Then came Jewish uprisings, not only in the Warsaw Ghetto but in scores of others, and in the death camps of Treblinka and Sobibor where Jewish members of the *Sonderkommando* in both places put to work on disposing of the corpses of the dead and sorting out their belongings succeeded at great cost to themselves in staging revolts and breaking out. Then there were the Jewish partisans who fought the Nazis from hiding places deep in the forests of eastern Europe. And finally, many thousands survived with false identity papers or were sheltered by their Gentile neighbours. For each and every one of them, survival itself was an act of resistance.

Orde Wingate was also correct: he could see the day when a Jewish army would emerge. The Jewish Brigade was a small part. And there is a fascinating thread between the men he trained in the Special Night Squads and the *Palmach* and the German Platoon, the SIG, X Troop, the Jewish Brigade and finally the Israel Defence Forces. Some warriors such as Israel Carmi fought in them all. Some of them fought in their war of independence and finally achieved their statehood.

British participation in this story is a mixed bag. With the publication of the April 1939 White Paper, London turned its back on the Balfour Declaration and was reluctant, for reasons of *realpolitik*, to raise a Jewish army in Palestine. On the other hand, men such as Bryan Hilton-Jones let his Jewish soldiers learn to fight like lions. They fought back against Hitler and helped create the foundations of the Israel Defence Forces. Anti-Semitism did exist in the British forces but it was not as rampant as in the French army. And it meant nothing to fighting men such as Hilton-Jones, Buck or Wingate.

The British authorities erred grievously in preventing so many aspiring Jewish warriors from fighting the Nazis and keeping them in the Pioneer Corps whilst the treatment of some refugees in the internment camps was despicable. Almost as bad was the long delay in rewarding with British citizenship after the war the foreign-born Jews who had fought in British special forces

How the British employed the German speakers was much better than the Russians and perhaps more effective than the Americans. It is a complex story and some of it is still secret.

Perhaps the American Jewish ex-servicemen caught the mood best in their novels. Herman Wouk, Joseph Heller, Norman Mailer and Leon Uris taught the Americans about the Second World War and the Holocaust through their best-selling novels.

The Brits got a lot wrong in the Second World War but the secret special forces were a big success. And it has been my pleasure to tell this story, including the part involving my native Wales. When I interviewed the 99-year old Myra Hayler in Aberdyfi her neighbour told me that she resolutely refused to believe the X troops were Jewish. I spoke to her in her house overlooking the beach where she recalled seeing amphibious vehicles training and I asked her in Welsh whether she minded that the soldiers were mainly Jewish. 'Of course not,' she said. 'They were our boys.' And so they were, even though they also helped to build the State of Israel.

Appendix 1

The Russian Experience

German Jews

After the Great War the parties of the right in Europe tended to be anti-Semitic whereas the left promised liberty and equality. The advent of Nazism drove many young German Jews into the arms of the communists. But they were not always encouraged in the underground in Germany because they posed a double security risk. Only a few hundred persisted because the communists were the most active opponents of Hitler until the 1939 pact with Moscow. Hundreds of young Jews also fought for the International Brigade in Spain. A handful of Jewish families of doctors and scientists as well as some socialist leaders were allowed into the USSR, but in the period of the great purges (1936–39) Stalin probably killed more communists than even Hitler managed in the whole Third Reich.

After Operation BARBAROSSA, nearly all the recent German immigrants, no matter how senior they were in the communist party, were deported to the far eastern regions. Some were permitted to return to Moscow in 1942/3 but the majority remained in the often frozen and nearly always starving conditions in the eastern regions until the end of the war.

A few very committed German communists were deployed in the Red Army as translators, though the majority were assigned to hard manual labour in the coal mines and in other parts of the Labour Army. A handful were trained as a pseudo unit of parachutists to infiltrate the Reich. Only one parachutist out of seventy sent actually escaped the Gestapo. The one who remained free passed as a Polish worker. Ten parachutists who survived the war as PoWs were sent, like many Russian prisoners, to slave camps in the USSR once they were repatriated. A few German-speaking Jews were also attached to partisan groups where their survival rates were higher. A small number of the children of prominent Jewish communists were used to produce German-language propaganda in Moscow or to work in German PoW camps as interrogators.

Although thousands of German Jewish intellectuals had fled to Russia in the 1930s, only eighty-three communists arrived back in Berlin in 1945 to work under the leadership of Walter Ulbricht; about 200 followed in the next two years. One of the most famous of the German émigrés to return was Marcus Wolf, who reached the No. 2 slot in the Stasi; he was the most famous and probably the most successful spymaster of the Cold War. His Jewish father, married to a Gentile, had been a doctor and a writer as well as being a prominent communist.

Russian Jews

Between 350,000 and 500,000 Jews served in the Red Army, compared with 550,000 in the American army, 100,000 in the Polish army and 30,000 in the British Army, according to the Yad Vashem archives. The figures are imprecise, partly because many Soviet Jews were listed under their nationalities, such as Latvian or Ukrainian. Many Jews initially joined the National Guard or local militias after the German invasion. Perhaps up to 140,000 were killed in the initial stages of the war because the militias were poorly trained and armed. A lot of Jewish servicemen and women were translators, physicians, and political officers.

Some became war correspondents. The most famous of all was Vasily Grossman, who came from a Ukrainian Jewish family from Kyiv. His coverage of the Great Patriotic War in the *Red Star*, the army newspaper, was widely read and admired. He wrote of the initial German advance where Heinkels and Junkers flying at night 'spread among the stars like lice'. It was at the turning point of the war, at Stalingrad, that Grossman honed his powers of description: 'the usual smell of the front line – a cross between a morgue and a blacksmith's'. He continued to report until the final Battle of Berlin. Grossman was later to become a brilliant, if banned, novelist.

Because of their often high academic standards, many of the Jewish fighters were officers serving as doctors, pilots and writers. But large numbers were also basic infantrymen, especially in the Lithuanian and Latvian forces. Despite the numerous alleged hostilities between Jews and Cossacks (and the alleged concept that Jews were not natural warriors) many Jews served in Cossack units, including reaching the levels of regimental commanders. Numerous Jews joined the partisans, including Holocaust survivors and Jews who had had false IDs in the occupied zones. Yet various attempts to set up a separate Jewish military formation got nowhere because of the Soviet propaganda purposes of the time. The Soviet education system and the wartime propaganda continually insisted there was no such entity as a Jewish nation and there never was and never could be a common destiny linking Soviet Jews, who were busy building a socialist world, and the decadent Jews of the rival capitalist states.

In contrast to Nazi policy, Russian women were encouraged to join the fight. The majority of Jewish women served in the medical field as doctors and nurses, while some worked as translators at the front as well. Jewish women also served in combat as pilots or navigators in the air force. Jewish fighters, male and female, were awarded a disproportionately high number of military distinctions. The highest was Hero of the Soviet Union, awarded to over 100 Jews, though this is an understated number because many were listed by their nationalities rather than their religion.

The Jewish Anti-Fascist Committee began work in the spring of 1942 and often highlighted Jews on the front line. The Committee also had a Yiddish newspaper, *Eynikayt*, that first appeared in June 1942. Many articles were syndicated to Jewish agencies and newspapers worldwide. Although the articles stressed the Jewish involvement in the overall war aims, they did explain that Jews had their own scores to settle with the invading Nazis. '*Far zayn foterland und zayn yidishn folk*': 'for their Soviet homeland and the Jewish people'. As the terrible details of the *Shoah* became known more and more, the ethnic consciousness of the Jewish fighters grew and motivated their determination to win the war.

In a powerful article, 'Jewish Combatants of the Red Army Confront the Holocaust,' Mordechai Altshuler noted the utter tragedy of returning soldiers trying to trace what happened to their whole families.[1] For reasons of field security, Red Army soldiers were not permitted to keep diaries, unless they had special permission as a correspondent or, in some cases, as a poet. Altshuler quotes Grossman who was just about to return to Kyiv. The tough correspondent wrote a letter to his wife in early 1944:

> They said that the city is completely devastated and only a few people, maybe a dozen out of many thousands, tens of thousands, of Jews who lived there, have survived. I have no hope of finding Mama alive. The only thing is I am hoping for is to find out about her last days and her death.

Sometimes returning Jewish veterans visited Gentile neighbours to find out what had happened; they would spot furniture and clothes which had been stolen from the Jewish family homes. Many of the soldiers were often moved to rediscover their Jewish roots, not least what was called the 'square letters' of the Hebrew alphabet. What was most disturbing, during the constant military victories of the last years of the war, was that many Russians, both soldiers and civilians, indulged in a xenophobic triumphalism that sometimes degenerated into traditional anti-Semitic slurs.

Many Red Army Jewish veterans retired to Israel after the break-up of the USSR. Most did not learn Hebrew and so few Israelis got to know their stories. Many claim to be living in poverty and say they get far less state pension than Holocaust survivors whose story is well known in Israel.

Soviet Germans

The term 'Soviet Germans' might appear to some to refer to the Russian Liberation Army under Andrey Vlasov, a Red Army general who defected to the Germans and helped create an army from Red Army PoWs and White Russians. The Germans also co-opted a large number of Cossacks.

This section refers, however to the one and half million ethnic Germans who lived in the USSR at the outbreak of war.

They were mainly the descendants of colonists who, in the late eighteenth century, were given permission by Empress Catherine the Great, herself a German, to settle in the Russian Empire. Most settled in the Volga region where, in 1923, an autonomous republic was established for them. Over 33,000 ethnic Germans were serving in the Red Army in 1939. At the start of the war, Soviet propaganda insisted on the difference between 'our Germans' and the Nazis and published stories of the many heroic actions by the local Germans. Official attitudes began to change as the Wehrmacht's savage thrusts moved ever more deeply into the USSR. Reports were circulated about ethnic Germans welcoming the Wehrmacht in some cases.

Stalin ordered that the ethnic Germans had to be transported to the east 'with a bang'. The autonomous republic was abolished and tens of thousands were despatched to Siberia, the Altai region and Kazakhstan. Many of the deportees were formed into so-called 'labour armies' engaged in coal mines, felling forests and construction. Soon even the best front-line German troops were removed from the Red Army.

Squadron Commander Pyotr Getts in his 1–16 fighter plane had singlehandedly chased away a squadron of enemy bombers over the city of Orsha in eastern Belarus.[2] He was awarded the Red Star decoration but it was eventually presented to him when he was working in the Urals as a tree-feller.[3] A few pulled rank and managed to stay in the army fighting at the front, especially if they could prove there were no possible replacements.

Ethnic Germans also proved extremely useful in partisan detachments. Their language skills were employed in sabotage and recce missions.

Wehrmacht defectors

A few hundred German soldiers willingly went over to the Russian side. Unsurprisingly, they were not trusted and were generally confined to the rear. An exception was Corporal Fritz Paul Schmenkel. He had been a long-term communist who had regularly gone AWOL and often served time in a military jail for his insubordination after he was forcibly conscripted in 1938. Schmenkel was born in Stettin and became a fervent communist when he was young, not least after his communist father was killed by Brownshirts in 1932. He deserted and joined the partisans to fight the Germans in occupied Belarus. He was captured by the Wehrmacht and executed in Minsk. Twenty years later he was made a Hero of the Soviet Union.

General Walter von Seydlitz-Kurzbach was a career officer from Prussian noble lineage. He thoroughly disagreed with Hitler's order not to break out from Stalingrad and so led some of his officers out of the encirclement and surrendered to the Russians. He campaigned to set up a German army in German uniform to fight Hitler but Stalin never trusted the concept. Seydlitz was used in Russian propaganda; nonetheless he did provide practical help to negotiate the surrender of the Germans at Königsberg in April 1945.

Though some Nazis believed in the existence of a real Seydlitz army, it never existed because Seydlitz never succeeded in creating a Soviet equivalent of Vlasov's Russian Liberation Army. It was a myth. In contrast, Romanian PoWs' request to create their own formations to fight alongside the Soviet Army was approved, and two Romanian infantry divisions were set up.

Still, the Nazis believed they had met and fought 'Seydlitz troops' as they called them. They were sure that the trophy Fw.190 and Bf.109 emblazoned with red stars used by Soviet pilots to scatter propagandistic leaflets and for reconnaissance missions were led by Seydlitz's German pilots.

Vlasov was hanged in Moscow in 1946 but Seydlitz received a Bundeswehr pension and died peacefully in his bed in West Germany in 1976.

Appendix 2

German Perspectives

G ermans deployed officers who could speak French and English in the West, not least for interrogating PoWs, especially in the lead up to D Day. They also developed a pseudo-strategy in the Battle of the Bulge in 1944.

Germans posing as Brits

The Germans fielded the 90th Light Afrika Division that served in North Africa and Italy. From this unit there merged the Division zbV Afrika (Africa Special Purposes Division). This amalgamated a number of special forces. Some were called Oasis companies, made up of men who were from Africa or had lived there. They were supposed to guard water supplies and especially oases. There were also raiders called *Sonderverband* 288 units.

The *Panzergrenadier-Regiment Afrika* was formed on 31 October 1942 and comprised some of the specialist units, including one locally-raised Arab battalion. Also, hundreds of former German soldiers in the French Foreign Legion were press-ganged into Wehrmacht service. Although the designation changed a number of times, it was called colloquially the Africa Division. It fought until the surrender in Tunisia; it was reformed in Sardinia during July 1943

The *Sonderverband* 288 (or SV 288) comprised of Germans from South West Africa and from South Africa, plus men who had worked in the area in the French Foreign Legion as well as oil workers who knew something of the Arab world. Some of the *Brandenburger* special forces were also recruited. They had specialised in behind-the-lines subversion, such as in Poland in the first waves of the invasion of Russia.

A designated English-speaking unit was formed – a company of about sixty men who could pass for English, or at least as Afrikaners from South Africa. Some could also speak Arabic as a handful had worked in Palestine. They were tasked with penetration roles and intelligence gathering. Some of the company were sent on a wild goose chase because the Germans believed that the Allies had a secret supply route which ran from the West Coast of Africa to the Red Sea. One group wore British uniforms and drove in captured British vehicles to pass for the LRDG. Three German groups separately traversed the Sahel, surviving in largely Free French territory, but it was a wasted effort as the Pan African Trunk Highway simply did not exist. The German desert SF units were also tasked by the Abwehr to transport German agents behind the lines to work in Egypt in Operation SALEM. The German unit got back to their lines but the two agents had been spotted and given an offer they could not refuse, and so were turned in Cairo.

Germans posing as Americans

This was an interesting example of a pseudo operation. Operation GREIF (not to be confused with an anti-partisan operation in August 1942 with the same name) was headed by Hitler's favourite special forces officer, Waffen SS *Obersturmbannführer* Otto Skorzeny. Often dubbed 'Hitler's last offensive' or the Battle of the Bulge, the German counter-offensive in December 1944 was initially tasked with capturing bridges over the Meuse river and then possibly pushing on to Antwerp. The idea was to divide the allies and possibly knock them out of the war, especially if their main supply route through Antwerp was disrupted. Hitler's generals disagreed with his plan to snatch victory from defeat but of course they did not tell him so. To saner military analysts, it seemed odd that Hitler should use up his few remaining resources to fight in the west and not the east.

A key component of Operation GREIF was the use of German troops dressed in UK and US uniforms, with captured Allied tanks and vehicles. They were supposed to spread confusion. Otto Skorzeny was Hitler's favourite because he had supervised the kidnapping of Miklós Horthy, the son of Admiral Horthy, Hungary's regent and prompted the father's resignation. He had also freed Mussolini from imprisonment during a daring mountain-top raid Operation EICHE.

Hitler told Skorzeny that he was giving him 'the most important mission in your career as a soldier'. The Führer added:

> I want you to create special units wearing American and British uniform. They will travel in captured Allied tanks. Think of the confusion you could cause! I envisage a whole string of false orders which will upset communications and attack morale.[1]

Hitler claimed that the Americans had deployed a similar deception at Aachen. The disguised GREIF force had to be capable of fraternising with American forces as they passed by. That required attention to authenticity in American accents, uniform and equipment.

The human cost of the deception plan was high, although Skorzeny calculated after the war that a mere eight men of 150 commandos in disguise were killed; only forty-four were active behind the lines during the main two weeks of the deception period. The Americans made grossly inflated claims about the number of Germans they had captured, indiscriminately counting any Germans found wearing an item of captured uniform, the American field jacket being an especially prized piece of kit in winter and at this late stage of the war. A conservative estimate of at least fifteen Germans disguised as Americans were executed by the US Army firing squads between December 1944 and mid-1945.

Skorzeny had only five to six weeks to organise the men and equipment. His request for English-speaking troops, preferably with an American accent, was passed on to every HQ on the Western Front and soon became known to the Allies. In the end only ten men could be found with first-language English and some knowledge of US idiom. US equipment was difficult too; only one functioning Sherman was found. Some German tanks and armoured cars were painted in US colours.

Nevertheless, Skorzeny led his special forces unit behind regular SS and Wehrmacht units. In his memoirs, Skorzeny maintained that one commando team entered Malmedy on 16 December and another persuaded one US unit to withdraw for Poteau on the same day. The small number of German English-speaking infiltrators did cause some chaos. Real US troops became obsessed by asking Trivial Pursuit-type questions about sports teams and state capitals. One US brigadier-general was held at gunpoint after he incorrectly said the Chicago Cubs were in the American League. How could he make such a mistake? In a number of incidents, some fatal, nervous military police opened fire on GIs. Rumours pulsated through the Allied ranks and soon General Eisenhower himself was isolated under strict security over Christmas because intelligence could not discount the story of Germans in US uniforms coming to kill or capture him; after all, Skorzeny was famous for such operations, wasn't he?

Some of his men were executed for violating the rules of war but at his trial in 1947 Skorzeny and nine of his officers were charged for wearing US uniforms. They were acquitted on the grounds that so long as he did not order his men to fight in combat while wearing US uniforms such a tactic was legitimate. An unusual witness at the trial was Wing Commander F.F.F. Yeo-Thomas who had worked in SOE under the code name of Tommy. He testified that he and his operatives wore German uniform behind enemy lines.

Skorzeny, during the war called the most dangerous man in Europe, fled from his internment camp in Germany to Spain where he mysteriously acquired a fortune, mainly as an arms dealer working with a strange mix of intelligence agencies, including the CIA. He was also close to some operatives in Mossad, and Israeli sources said he was paid to kill a leading Nazi fugitive from justice. Paradoxically, Skorzeny was reputed to have been central in the Odessa organisation that sent top Nazis to South America (although some historians claim that Odessa was a myth). Skorzeny did make millions selling arms and working to train Arab forces. One alleged beneficiary of his SS skills was Yasser Arafat. In 1942 the then Lieutenant Anwar Sadat was in touch with Rommel and the future Egyptian president worked with Skorzeny. The Austrian-born SS-Obersturmbannführer died in Madrid, where he had become a celebrity, in 1975.[2]

Legion of St George

The Legion of St George, later officially called the British Free Corps, was similar in some ways (and very dissimilar in others) to the Special Interrogation Group. They were foreigners dressed in German uniform and their size and longevity were similar. They were not a pseudo unit, however, but rather intended to be an integral part of the Wehrmacht fighting on the Eastern Front. According to Adrian Weale, around fifty-four men joined the Free Corps that never had a standing strength of more than twenty-seven men.[3] The idea for the Corps came from John Amery, a British fascist, and the son of the Secretary of State for India, Leo Amery. John Amery travelled to Berlin in October 1942 to set up a unit similar to the Legion of French Volunteers against Bolshevism. He made pro-German broadcasts and toured PoW camps.

The British Free Corps was finally formed in January 1944, but it was not until the end of 1944 that the unit was based in Dresden to be trained by the Waffen SS. They did not get near the Eastern Front until March 1945, briefly on the west bank of the Oder River. The various German fighting units they were attached to did not seem to know what to do with these Brits, who were viewed with some suspicion. They were eventually ordered to make their way west to surrender to the Americans. The last two Brits in German SS uniform surrendered on 2 May 1945.

The last defenders of Berlin in April 1945 wore the uniforms of the Wehrmacht, but a lot of them were foreigners. Many were Frenchmen from the SS Charlemagne Division who had fought all the way from Russia. Others were Scandinavians from the Nordland Division. Spaniards, Estonians and Latvians who had joined their respective SS national units were still fighting hard as the Red Army swallowed the Nazi capital. More Dutchmen had carried arms for Hitler, some 25,000, of whom 10,000 were killed, than wore the khaki of the Free

Netherlands forces. With the rag-tag array of foreigners defending Berlin was a slightly older soldier, blind in one eye; he was actually German, born in Shanghai, but on his right arm he wore the Union Jack. This was Wilhelm August Rössler, one of the last Free Corps men on his feet and holding a weapon.[4]

Some of the 2,000 Indians who joined the Nazis were often sick of being PoWs although many were also nationalists. And the Germans thought of setting up an Irish unit made up of anti-British nationalists too. Throughout military history it was common to employ units of foreign mercenaries. George III deployed Hessian mercenaries, Napoleon maintained his Polish Lancers and the Pope has his Swiss Guard. Even today the British maintain their highly respected Gurkhas and the French still deploy their Foreign Legion throughout Africa. The German system of using foreign fighters was not connected to material advantage; they were mainly inspired by a fervent anti-communism. One of the key planks of Nazi propaganda was the 'European Crusade against Bolshevism'. And Bolsheviks and Jews were often conflated.

At their courts martial, several of the former Free Corps men claimed that they joined to gather intelligence on the Germans and intended to disrupt their activities. No officers actually joined the Free Corps, and it was technically commanded by English-speaking German SS officers. Very briefly, a British officer was released from a German mental hospital, but he was not fit to be even a propaganda frontman and, anyway, refused to put on the Free Corps uniform.

The founding father of the unit, John Amery, was condemned for treason. Albert Pierrepoint, the executioner, came for Amery on the morning of 29 December 1945. The trial had lasted just eight minutes because Amery had pleaded guilty to avoid embarrassing his eminent family with a long trial. When the executioner entered Amery's cell in Wandsworth Jail, the prisoner rose and said: 'I have always wanted to meet you but not, of course, in these circumstances.' Pierrepoint wrote in his memoirs that 'Amery was the bravest man he had ever hanged'.

Glossary of Terms

Abwehr	German military intelligence organisation that concentrated on human intelligence.
Aliyah	A 'wave' of Jewish migration to Palestine from the diaspora. The first was 1882–1904, the second 19014–1914 and then a general wave of migrants from 1914–1948
Anschluss	German annexation of Austria (1938)
Bricha	(also *Bericha*) Movement An organisation to help Jewish survivors in Europe to emigrate to Palestine
DSO	Distinguished Service Order
Fauda	An Israeli TV series about Jewish special forces who often pretend to be Arabs
43 Group	Jewish group set up in London at end of the Second World War to combat British fascists
Hachsharot	Camps for agricultural training before migration to Palestine
Haganah	The underground Jewish army in the Mandate
Irgun	Jewish paramilitary organisation that operated in Palestine from 1931–1948. Often violent and anti-British
Judenstaat	Jewish homeland
Kapo	A prisoner in a Nazi camp who was assigned by the *Schutzstaffel* (SS) guards to supervise forced labour or carry out administrative tasks
Knesset	The Israeli parliament
Kibbutz	Jewish agricultural settlement based on cooperative principles

Kosher	Food prepared according to Jewish dietary laws
The Mandate	Palestine was part of the territory mandated to Britain by the League of Nations in 1923. Britain administered the territory west of the Jordan River until Israel declared independence
MC	Military Cross, gallantry award issued to officers and warrant officers
MM	Military Medal, gallantry award for non-commissioned ranks
Morgenthau Plan	A proposal to eliminate Germany's ability to wage war following the Second World War by eliminating its arms industry and removing or destroying other key industries basic to military strength
Nakam	Jewish revenge groups; also called *Dam Yisrael Noter* ('the blood of Israel avenges'; the acronym DIN also means 'judgement')
NKVD	Soviet secret police set up in 1917
Nokmim	Jewish Avengers
Palmach	Jewish elite commandos during the Mandate
Pogroms	Anti-Jewish riots and destruction of Jewish properties
Raj	British-ruled India
sabra	Jew born in Israel
Shoah	Holocaust
Sonderkommando	Jews who were given slightly special treatment for disposing of the dead in the camps especially in the crematoria
Special Night Squads	A counter-insurgency unit set up in Palestine by Orde Wingate that operated in the late 1930s
TTG	(*Tilhas Tizig Gesheften* – literally 'kiss my arse business'; unofficial Jewish revenge killings of senior Nazis
Torah	The first five books of the Hebrew Bible
War of Independence	Jewish fight to set up Israel. The Palestinian Arabs refer to it as the *Nakbah*, catastrophe
Werewolves	A German resistance movement active in 1945–46

Yishuv	The Jewish settlements in the Mandate run by their own semi-official organisations
Zionism	The desire of Jews to return to live in Palestine/Israel and to govern themselves
Z officers	British stool pigeons in PoW camps

Abbreviations

ATS	Auxiliary Territorial Service
CSDIC	Combined Services Detailed Interrogation Centre
DAK	*Deutsches Afrikakorps* (later part of *Panzerarmee Afrika* of Italian and German forces)
DP	Displaced person
FANY	First Aid Nursing Yeomanry
LRDG	Long Range Desert Group
MI5	The Security Service, also known as MI5 (Military Intelligence, Section 5), is the United Kingdom's domestic counter-intelligence and security agency and is part of its intelligence machinery alongside the Secret Intelligence Service (MI6), which operates abroad
MI8	The Radio Security Service, under the War Office in the Second World War
MI9	A Division of the Directorate of Military Intelligence involved in helping escaping Allied troops to return to Britain
MII9	The Military Intelligence Division in charge of obtaining information from PoWs
MTB	Motor Torpedo Boat
NCO	Non-Commissioned Officer
OSS	Office of Strategic Services
PoW	Prisoner of War
PPA	Popski's Private Army
SAS	Special Air Service
SBS	Special Boat Section
SD	*Sicherheitsdienst*
SIG	Special Interrogation Group

SIS	Secret Intelligence Service
SOE	Special Operations Executive
SS	*Schutzstaffel*
SSRF	Small Scale Raiding Force
WAAF	Women's Auxiliary air Force
ZOB	Jewish Combat Organisation
ZZW	Jewish Military Union

The main Jewish forces featured in this book

The Zion Mule Corps (1915–1916)
The Jewish Legion (1917–21)
Haganah (1920–48)/*Palmach* (1941–48)
Irgun (1931–1948)
The German Platoon (1942–45)
The Special Interrogation Group (1942)
X Troop (1942–45)
Jewish Brigade (1944–46)
Israel Defence Forces (1948–)

Notes

Chapter 1: The first modern Jewish armies

1. See Martin Sugarman, 'The Zion Muleteers of Gallipoli', Jewish Virtual Library. I must thank Martin Sugarman for pointing out the role of Sarah Aaronsohn and the NILI spy ring. NILI is an acronym which stands for the Hebrew phrase *Netzah Yisrael Lo Yeshaker*, which translates as 'the Eternal One of Israel will not lie'. Sarah was perhaps the first *Sabra* female martyr for Zionism. She was born and died in Zichon Yaakov where her Romanian Zionist family had moved in the first *Aliyah*. She and her immediate family worked tirelessly with the British to undermine the Turkish war effort. She was captured and she and her family were brutally tortured. She was so badly hurt that she shot herself in October 1917. British intelligence called her group of forty agents the 'A Organization' because it was so important and the biggest in the Middle East.
2. Edward Erickson, *Ordered to Die: A History of the Ottoman Army in the First World War* (Greenwood, Westpoint, 2001) p. 200.
3. Rafael Medoff, *Militant Zionism in America: the rise and impact of the Jabotinsky movement* (University of Alabama, Tuscaloosa, 2002) p. 90. See also Jan Láníček and James Jordan, Editors, *Governments in Exile and the Jews During the Second World war* (Vallentine Mitchell, London, 2021) p. 5.
4. There is less agreement on the reasons for this lack of action (helping Jews). Some have seen it as the consequences of the hostility of policy-makers, particularly leading civil servants, to the Jews, exacerbated in the Foreign Office by the belief that Jewish leaders in the West were exploiting the sufferings of their co-religionists to advance a Zionist agenda. Others have cited the fear of governments of popular anti-Semitism and that the war might be seen as being fought for Jewish interests and the widespread indifference to the fate of the Jews.
5. Ken Delve, *Disaster in the Desert: An Alternate History of El Alamein and Rommel's North Africa Campaign* (Greenhill Books, Barnsley, 2019). For another related counter-factual see John Keegan, 'How Hitler Could have won the war' in Robert Cowley, Editor, *What If? Military Historians Imagine What Might Have Been* (Pan, London, 2001).

Chapter 2: The Special Interrogation Group

1. Ironically, many of the senior Nazis had a record of protecting the 'good' Jews they knew. Even Hitler ordered the Gestapo to safeguard an Austrian Jewish doctor who had helped his mother. Eduard Bloch had tended to Hitler's beloved mother, Klara, when she was dying of cancer. Dr Bloch had practised in Linz and had treated the whole family, including Adolf Hitler, often at a very reduced rate because of the family's penury. When Klara died, Hitler offered Bloch his 'everlasting gratitude'. According to Bloch, Klara was a 'very pious and kind woman'. *'Sie würde sich im Grabe herumdrehen, wenn sie wüsste, was aus ihm geworden ist.'* That was Bloch's judgement: she would turn in her grave if she could know what became of him. Hitler kept to his word and sometimes asked after Bloch after the Anschluss. Bloch was given a special status by the Gestapo, an 'Edeljude' – a noble Jew, the only one with such a status in Linz. Although Bloch had to stop his practice he and his wife were left alone in their house and not hassled when they arranged to emigrate to the USA in 1940, although they could take less than 20 marks with them.

2. For a detailed analysis of military intelligence operations with Italian PoWs, see Bob Moore and Kent Fedorowich, *The British Empire and Italian Prisoners of War (1940–47)* (Palgrave Macmillan, London, 2002). For some of the intelligence background on the SIG, see The National Archives: WO 218/159, 17 March 1942. Also, TNA: WO 201/727.

3. Lengthy interviews (2012) with RAF Flight Sergeant Leslie Moorcraft, who serviced the main fighters on the island for three years.

4. Another version has Brückner decorated by Rommel. In this version he soldiered on with the *Afrikakorps* but was captured a second time, by the Americans this time. And then he was said to have re-joined the French Foreign Legion and fought in the Algerian war. The numerous aliases in this story often undermine accurate historical analysis.

Chapter Three: The Raid on Tobruk

1. Two Hollywood films were made that very loosely related to Operation AGREEMENT. In 1967 Rock Hudson and George Peppard starred in *Tobruk*. The mission in this version was a great success. It is interesting, however, because it does feature the SIG quite prominently. A B-movie made in 1971, called *Raid on Rommel* and starring Richard Burton, used some of the battle scenes from the more expensive predecessor.

2. Again, I would like to thank Martin Sugarman not only for lengthy discussions, but for the original research in his master work. In this case I am indebted to his chapter 'Lions of Judah: The Jewish Commandos of the SIG' in Martin Sugarman, *Fighting Back: British Jewry's Military Contribution in the Second World War* (Vallentine Mitchell, London, 2017) pp. 185–209.

3. Sugarman, p. 201. See also the very lively Boy's Own account by Gordon Landsborough, *Tobruk Commando: The Raid to Destroy Rommel's Base*

(Frontline Books, Barnsley, 2015). The problem with the Landsborough version is that the original was produced in 1956 and many of the details were still secret and so often aliases were deployed – for example, Buck is referred to as Bray.

4. John Sadler, *Operation Agreement: Jewish Commandos and the Raid on Tobruk* (Osprey, Oxford, 2016) pp. 208 and 224.
5. See Janusz Piekalkiewicz, *Rommel und die Geheimdienste in Nordafrika (1941–1943)* (FA Herbig, Munich, 1992). The British had been penetrating Rommel's signals via the so-called 'Ultra'. Ultra enabled Churchill to find out that Hitler had deferred Operation SEALION and this permitted the British leader to throw more troops into Egypt at the right time. Rommel's most important intelligence source, besides his own excellent theatre intercepts, was provided by what the German leader called *die gute Quelle*. This meant the cables sent to Washington by the Anglophobic Colonel Bonner Frank Feller, the US military attaché in Cairo. Unwittingly, the American provided detailed data for Rommel.
6. For details on Charlie Coles's comments on Buck, see David Jefferson, *Tobruk: A Raid Too Far* (Hale, London, 2013) pp. 248–89.
7. Anders Lassen VC MC and Two Bars, was a highly decorated Danish soldier who was posthumously awarded Britain's highest gallantry award for his actions during Operation ROAST on 8 April 1945 at Lake Comácchio in Italy in the final weeks of the Italian campaign.

Chapter 4: The X Troop

1. Leah Garrett, *X Troop: The Secret Jewish Commandos who helped defeat the Nazis* (Chatto and Windus, London 2021).
2. Author's interview 26 May 2022. Myra Hayler insisted there was never any trouble in the village with the X Troopers. 'They were always very well-behaved,' she said.
3. Peter Masters, *Striking Back: A Jewish Commando's War against the Nazis,* (Presidio, Novato, California, 1997).
4. Antony Beevor, *Arnhem: The Battles for the Bridges, 1944* (Penguin, London, 2019) p. 276.
5. I am grateful to Nerys Pipkin, The Skipper's daughter, for being able to quote from her father's correspondence.
6. For a list of who served in the X Troop, with their original and assumed *noms de guerre*, see Chapter 14 of Martin Sugarman, *Fighting Back* (Vallentine Mitchell, London, 2017).

Chapter 5: The Ritchie Boys

1. Bruce Henderson, *The Ritchie Boys: The Jews who Escaped the Nazis and Returned to Fight Hitler* (William Collins, London, 2017) p. 113. I am indebted to Henderson's impressive research, and also his correspondence

with me (April 2021) which confirmed my views on the lack of US-UK cooperation on intelligence training.

2. Ibid., p. 159.
3. *Volksgrenadier* was the name given to a type of German division formed in late 1944 after the double loss of Army Group Centre to the Soviet meatgrinder and Fifth Panzer Army in Normandy. The title itself was intended to build morale appealing to nationalism (*Volk*) and the older military traditions (*Grenadier*). Berlin formed seventy-eight such replacement divisions during the war. They were professional military units with standardised weapons, despite the hotch-potch of personnel mixing veterans, recently wounded, older men plus Luftwaffe and unused naval assets. They were quite distinct from the *Volkssturm* militia.
4. *Ritchie Boys*, p. 295.
5. *Ritchie Boys*, p. 234.
6. The *Sicherheitsdienst des Reichsführers-SS* (Security Service of the Reichsführer-SS), or SD, was the intelligence agency of the SS and the Nazi Party in Nazi Germany. Originating in 1931, the organisation was the first Nazi intelligence organisation to be established.
7. Arnold Kramer, *Nazi Prisoners of War in America* (Lyons Press, Lanham, MD, 2020) p. 257.
8. See the unorthodox view in Peter den Hertog, *Why did Hitler Hate the Jews?* (Pen and Sword, Barnsley, 2020).

Chapter 6: And they also served …
1. Howard Blum, *The Jewish Brigade* (Perennial, New York, 2002) p. 4.
2. I am indebted, as ever, to Martin Sugarman. See his *Fighting Back* (Valentine Mitchell, London, 2017) pp. 48–54.
3. Again, Martin Sugarman has battled with the archives to produce a useful summary, see *Fighting Back*, pp. 82–105.
4. *Fighting Back*, p. 94.
5. Robert Philpot, 'How Britain's German-born Jewish "secret listeners" helped win World War II', *The Times of Israel*, 1 November 2019. This lengthy article is a review of Helen Fry's informative book, *The Walls Have Ears* (Yale University Press, London, 2020). See also, Sönke Neitzel and Harald Welzer, *Soldaten* (Simon and Schuster, London, 2012).
6. The Home Guard had an umbrella role for various secret organisations. The Auxiliary Units or GHQ Auxiliary Units were volunteers who wore Home Guard uniforms but would take action only after the conventional phase of regular army and Home Guard defence during an invasion. They were not intended to be a long-term secret resistance, rather they would fight on and cause maximum disruption immediately after the conventional forces had retreated or surrendered. Their life expectancy was about 12 days. This was run by the War Office and was separate from the SIS (MI6) civilian Home

Defence Scheme. Colloquially the members of the Auxiliary Units were called 'scallywags' and their resistance roles were dubbed 'scallywagging'. Some the auxiliaries were formed into Operational Patrols, often farmers and landowners. Particularly valued were gamekeepers and poachers. About 3,600 men were specially trained in guerrilla warfare. Each cell was expected to be autonomous and work within a 15-mile radius of their OBs (Operational Bases). Some 500 were built by Royal Engineers, usually in woodland. They also prepared OPs (Observation Points) and ammunition stores. They were expected to shoot themselves rather than be taken alive. As the British conventional forces fell back to pre-prepared defence lines, they would conduct extensive sabotage. One of their jobs was to assassinate senior German officers and so the patrol groups secretly reconnoitred local country houses that might be commandeered by the German army and lists of selected fifth columnists had been drawn up for early killing. The secret troops were sometimes used to guard against German commando raiders (for example to protect the Pluto fuel pipeline on the Isle of Wight prior to D-Day) but were stood down with the rest of the Home Guard in November 1944.

Chapter 7: Resistance

1. Halik Kochanski, *Resistance: the Underground War in Europe 1939–45* (Penguin, London, 2022) p. 141. This is a very recent and magisterial work on the subject.
2. Ibid., p. 299.
3. Ibid., p. 304.
4. Judy Batalion, *The Light of Days: Women Fighters of the Jewish Resistance* (Virago, London, 2020) p. 3.
5. Judith Tydor Baumel-Schwartz, *Perfect Heroes: The World War Two Parachutists and the Making of Israeli Collective Memory* (University of Wisconsin, Wisconsin, 2010).
6. Martin Sugarman, *Fighting Back* (Vallentine Mitchell, London, 2017) p. 380.

Chapter 8: Revenge

1. Howard Blum, *The Brigade* (Perennial, New York, 2002) p. 150.
2. Harald Jähner, *Aftermath: Life in the Fallout of the Third Reich, 1945–55* (W.H. Allen, London, 2021).
3. Ibid., p. 136.
4. Helen Fry, *The King's Most Loyal Enemy Aliens: The Germans who Fought for Britain in the Second World War* (Sutton, Stroud, 2007) p. 201.
5. Ibid., pp. 204–5.
6. Blum, *The Brigade* op cit., p. 185.
7. A dramatised version of the story can be found in Damien Lewis, *SAS Nazi Hunters: The Ultra-Secret Unit and the Hunt for Hitler's War Criminals*

(Quercus, London, 2015). See also, Anthony Kemp, *The Secret Hunters* (Coronet, Sevenoaks, 1988).

8. Ibid., p. 18.
9. Ibid., p. 267.
10. Sarah Helms, *A Life in Secrets: Vera Atkins and the lost agents of the SOE* (Abacus, London, 2006) p. xxii.
11. In 1939 the Artists Rifles had been redesignated 163 (Officer Cadet Training Unit) OCTU. Although some authorities state that they became 56th Reconnaissance Regiment, this never happened, although it had been proposed. On 1 January 1947 the Artists Rifles were reconstituted as a TA infantry unit but in July 1947 were transferred to the Army Air Corps as 21st Special Air Service Regiment. In May 1950 it was transferred to the Corps of the SAS Regiment as 21st Special Air Service Regiment (Artists Rifles). The disbanded wartime SAS regiments had been part of the Army Air Corps from 1944 until disbandment. In 1950 the Malayan Scouts were raised in Malaya by Lieutenant Colonel J.M. 'Mike' Calvert but re-organised in 1952 as 22nd SAS Regiment. A 23rd SAS Regiment was formed in London in 1959.

Appendix 1: The Russian Experience

1. Mordechai Altshuler, 'Jewish Combatants of the Red Army Confront the Holocaust' in Harriet Murav and Genady Estraikh, Editors, *Soviet Jews in the World War Two: Fighting, Witnessing, Remembering* (Academic Studies Press, Boston, 2014) pp. 16–35.
2. The Polikarpov I-16 was a Soviet single-engine single-seat fighter aircraft of revolutionary design; it was the world's first low-wing cantilever monoplane fighter with retractable landing gear to attain operational status.
3. Boris Egorov, 'How Germans fought for the USSR in World War Two', *Russia Beyond*, 10/2/21 https://www.rbth.com/history/333384-how-germans-fought-for-ussr

Appendix 2: German Perspectives

1. Stuart Smith, *Otto Skorzeny: The Devil's Disciple* (Osprey, Oxford, 2018) p. 163. See also *Otto Skorzeny, Hitler's Commando: The Daring Missions of Otto Skorzeny and the Nazi Special Forces* (Pen and Sword, Barnsley, 2011). German intelligence was also trying to organise a mass break-out of German PoWs in Britain to coincide with the Battle of the Bulge. They were supposed to mass and stage a march on London to create a security risk of massive proportions. This is according to Charles Whiting's perhaps dubious account, *The March on London* (Leo Cooper, London, 1992).
2. One of the very best accounts of the December 1944 campaign is Peter Caddick-Adams, *Snow and Steel: Battle of the Bulge* (Preface, London, 2014). For post-war details on Skorzeny see pp. 707–8.

3. Adrian Weale, *Renegades: Hitler's Englishmen* (Warner, London, 1994). See also Ronald Seth, *Jackals of the Reich: The First Full Account of Hitler's British Korps* (New English Library, London, 1972) says around 100 British PoWs went through the ranks of the Corps.

4. Weale, p. 6. One of the most interesting foreign collaborators with the Germans was Leon Degrelle. He was a French-speaking Belgian politician who had no military training until he decided to join as a private, aged 35, the Belgian unit that became the 28th SS Division *Wallonie*. He ended up commanding the unit and became the first non-German to be awarded the Oak Leaves to the Knight's Cross of the Iron Cross. Hitler said to him, 'If I had a son, I would wish him to be like you.' Degrelle also escaped at the end of the war to Spain where he died in 1994. See his *The Eastern Front: Memoirs of a Waffen SS Volunteer, 1941–1945* (Institute for Historical Review, Newport Beach, CA, 1993).

Select Bibliography

Altshuler, Mordechai, 'Jewish Combatants of the Red Army Confront the Holocaust' in Harriet Murav and Genady Estraikh, eds., *Soviet Jews in the World War Two: Fighting, Witnessing, Remembering* (Academic Studies Press, Boston, 2014) pp. 16–35.

Batalion, Judy, *The Light of Days: Women Fighters of the Jewish Resistance* (Virago, London, 2020).

Baumel-Schwartz, Judith Tydor, *Perfect Heroes: The World War Two Parachutists and the Making of Israeli Collective Memory* (University of Wisconsin, Wisconsin, 2010).

Beckman, Morris, *The Jewish Brigade: An Army with Two Masters* (Spellmount, Stroud, 2009).

Beevor, Antony, *Arnhem: The Battles for the Bridges, 1944* (Penguin, London, 2019).

Bishop, Patrick, *Operation Jubilee: Dieppe, 1942* (Viking, London, 2021).

Blume, Howard, *The Brigade* (Perennial, New York, 2002).

Braddock, David, *Britain's Desert war in Egypt and Libya 1940–1942* (Pen and Sword, Barnsley, 2019).

Caddick-Adams, Peter, *Monty and Rommel: Parallel Lives* (Preface, London, 2011).

——, *Snow and Steel: The Battle of the Bulge* (Preface, London, 2014).

Cesarani, David, *Major Farran's Hat* (Vintage, London, 2010).

Cobain, Ian, *Cruel Britannia: A Secret History of Torture* (Portobello, London, 2012).

Dear, Ian, *Ten Commando 1942–1945* (Leo Cooper, London, 1987).

Den Hertog, Peter, *Why Did Hitler Hate the Jews?* (Frontline, Barnsley, 2020).

Downing, Taylor, *1942: Britain at the Brink* (Little, Brown, London, 2022).

Evans, Richard, *The Hitler Conspiracies: The Third Reich and the Paranoid Imagination* (Allen Lane, London, 2020).

Fry, Helen, *The King's Most Loyal Enemy Aliens* (Sutton, Stroud, 2007).

——, *German Schoolboy, British Commando* (History Press, Stroud, 2010).

——, *The Walls Have Ears* (Yale University Press, London, 2020).

Garrett, Leah, *X Troop: The Secret Commandos Who Helped Defeat the Nazis* (Chatto and Windus, London, 2021).

Grossman, Vasily, *A Writer at War: Vasily Grossman with the Red Army, 1941–1945* ((Pimlico, London, 2006).

Harris, Paul, 'The Germans who Fled and Fought Hitler for us', *Daily Mail*, 5 September 2007.

Hawes, Stephen and Ralph White, *Resistance in Europe: 1939–45* (Penguin, Middlesex, 1976).

Henderson, Bruce, *The Ritchie Boys* (William Collins, London, 2017).

Jefferson, David, *Tobruk: A Raid Too Far* (Hale, London, 2013).

Keene, Tom, *Cloak of enemies: Churchill's SOE, Enemies at home and the 'Cockleshell Heroes'* (Spellmount, Stroud, 2012).

Kemp, Anthony, *The Secret Hunters* (Coronet, Sevenoaks, 1988).

King, Gilbert 'The Monocled World War Two Interrogator', *Smithsonian Magazine*, 23 November 2011.

Kochanski, Halik, *Resistance: The Underground War in Europe 1939–45* (Penguin, London, 2022).

Kramer, Arnold, *Nazi Prisoners of War in America* (Lyons Press, Guilford, Connecticut, 2020).

Lacqueur, Walter, *Generation Exodus: The Fate of Young Jewish Refugees from Nazi Germany* (I B Tauris, London, 2004).

Landsborough, Gordon, *Tobruk Commando: The Raid to Destroy Rommel's Base* (Frontline Books, Barnsley, 2015).

Lane, Colonel George, obituary *Daily Telegraph*, 26 March 2010.

Láníček, Jan and James Jordan, *Governments-in-Exile and the Jews during the Second World War* (Vallentine Mitchell, London, 2013).

Leasor, James, *Green Beach* (Self-published, London, 1975).

Lee, Eric, *Operation Basalt: The British Raid on Sark* (History Press, Stroud, 2017).

Lewis, Damien, *Churchill's Secret Warriors* (Quercus, London, 2014).

——, *SAS Ghost Patrol: The Ultra-Secret Unit that posed as Nazi Stormtroopers,* (Quercus, London, 2017).

——, *SAS Nazi Hunters* (Quercus, London, 2019).

Maclean, Fitzroy, *Eastern Approaches* (Penguin, London, 2019).

Marnham, Patrick, *War in the Shadows: Resistance, Deception and Betrayal in Occupied France* (Oneworld, London, 2021).

Marks, Leo, *Between Silk and Cyanide: A Code-maker's War 1941–45* (History Press, Stroud, 2007).

Masters, Peter, *Striking Back: A Jewish Commando's War against the Nazis,* (Presidio, Novato, California, 1997).

Medoff, Rafael, *Militant: The Rise and Impact of Zionism; the Jabotinsky Movement in America* (University of Alabama, Tuscaloosa, 2002).

Messenger, Charles, *The Middle East Commandos* (William Kimber, Wellingborough, UK, 1988).

Moorcraft, Paul, *Dying for the Truth: The Concise History of Frontline War Reporting* (Pen and Sword, Barnsley, 2016).

Moore, Deborah Dash, *GI Jews: How World War II changed a Generation* (Harvard University Press, Cambridge Massachusetts, 2006).

Morris, Eric, *Guerrillas in Uniform* (Hutchinson, London, 1989).

Morris, Henry, *We Will Remember Them* (Brassey's, London, 1989).

Neitzel, Sönke and Harald Welzer, *Soldaten* (Simon and Schuster, London, 2012).

O'Carroll, Brendan, *The Long Range Desert Group in Action (1940–1943)* (Pen and Sword, Barnsley, 2020).

Owen, David Lloyd, *The Long Range Desert Group (1940–1945)* (Pen and Sword, Barnsley, 2011).

Parkin, Simon. *The Island of Extraordinary Captives* (Sceptre, London, 2022).

Philpot, Robert, 'How Britain's German-born Jewish "secret listeners" helped win World War II', *The Times of Israel*, 1 November 2019.

Piekalkiewicz, Janusz, *Rommel und die Geheimdienste in Nordafrika (1941–1943)* (F.A. Herbig, Munich, 1992).

Sadler, John, *Operation Agreement: Jewish Commandos and the Raid on Tobruk* (Osprey, Oxford, 2016).

Shlaim, Avi, *The Iron Wall: Israel and the Arab World* (Penguin, London, 2014).

Smith, Peter, *Massacre at Tobruk* (Stackpole, Mechanicsburg PA, 2008).

Smith, Stuart, *Otto Skorzeny: The Devil's Disciple* (Osprey, Oxford, 2018).

Sugarman, Martin, *Fighting Back: British Jewry's Military Contribution in the Second World War* (Vallentine Mitchell, London, 2017).

Van der Bijl, Nick, *Commandos in Exile* (Pen and Sword, Barnsley, 2008).

Van Tonder, Gerry, *Irgun* (Pen and Sword, Barnsley, 2019).

Index